ALCOHOL USE AND ALCOHOLISM

GARLAND REFERENCE LIBRARY
OF SOCIAL SCIENCE
(VOL. 350)

ALCOHOL USE AND ALCOHOLISM
A Guide to the Literature

Penny Booth Page

GARLAND PUBLISHING, INC. • NEW YORK & LONDON
1986

Library of Congress Cataloging-in-Publication Data

Page, Penny Booth, 1949–
Alcohol use and alcoholism.

(Garland reference library of social science ; 350)
Includes indexes.
1. Alcoholism—United States—Bibliography.
2. Drinking of alcoholic beverages—United States—
Bibliography. I. Title. II. Series.
Z7721.P33 1986 [HV5292] 016.362.2′92′0973 83-49073
ISBN 0-8240-9020-9

Cover design by Alison Lew

Printed on acid-free, 250-year-life paper
Manufactured in the United States of America

To Mark
with love and thanks

CONTENTS

Acknowledgements

This volume would not have been possible without the help and encouragement of several people. My good friend Mary Weathers labored many long and arduous hours entering the manuscript into her word processor. Dawood Farahi lent his technical expertise to help me overcome several formatting problems. The staff at the Center of Alcohol Studies Library (Janet Pichette, Chris Maier, Sylvia Falk, and Pei-lan Chen) managed the library while I was absent on leave preparing the final manuscript. And most importantly, my husband, Mark Lender, provided technical assistance, enthusiasm, and patient encouragement to keep me going over the rough spots. Thank you all.

INTRODUCTION

Alcohol use and alcohol problems have been part of the social fabric of the United States since the first European colonists arrived. Indeed, these early settlers felt that regular, moderate alcohol use helped ward off chills, disease, and fatigue. Imported European beers and spirits were soon joined by American-made whiskeys, rum, and cider. Consumption levels rose from 5.8 gallons of absolute alcohol per person in 1790 to 7.1 gallons by 1830 (as contrasted with 2.8 gallons today), and as consumption levels increased so did the incidence of public intoxication and chronic drunkenness.[1]

Perhaps the first alcohol public awareness campaign was conducted by the American Temperance Movement--actually a variety of organizations and societies (including the American Temperance Society, the Washingtonians, the Sons of Temperance, the Woman's Christian Temperance Union, the Anti-Saloon League, the Prohibition Party, and others). The first groups started in the early decades of the nineteenth century and advocated the temperate use of the so-called weaker alcoholic beverages (beer, ale, wine, cider); thus they became known as "Temperance" groups. It was not until the 1830s that these groups and their successors decided that alcohol in any form was the problem and that abstention from all alcoholic beverages was the way to prevent the spread of chronic inebriation. Thus began one of the most effective propaganda campaigns dealing with alcohol problems in this country. Using literature, theater, artwork, and public oratory, the Temperance Movement decried the debilitating effects of alcohol on the brain, the body, behavior, family relationships, and security. By the time National Prohibition began in 1920, there was, in fact, widespread consensus on the need for such action.

Although National Prohibition was not a success (largely for reasons of enforcement), it was not a complete failure. Consumption levels and alcohol-related arrests, hospitalizations, and deaths declined significantly.[2] After

Prohibition was repealed in 1933, Americans were left without a public consensus or policy regarding alcohol use. As consumption levels and alcohol problems began to climb again, a group of scientists formed the Research Council on Problems of Alcohol to sponsor research on the effects of alcohol use on the individual. Though the Council was short-lived, other scientists and institutions, most notably the Yale Center of Alcohol Studies (later at Rutgers), began research on alcohol use and alcohol problems. The National Committee for Education on Alcoholism (which later became the National Council on Alcoholism) was founded in 1944 to provide public information and referral for alcohol problems. In 1971 the federal government established the National Institute on Alcohol Abuse and Alcoholism to conduct and to fund research, education, and dissemination of information about all aspects of alcohol use.

The current approach to alcohol use and its consequences is based on research and public education. As our understanding about alcohol has increased, so has our understanding of the depth and scope of alcohol problems. We now know that alcohol is involved in approximately 50% of all motor vehicle deaths, 35-40% of all suicides, and 50% of all homicides.[3] Research studies have shown that alcohol is a significant factor in serious crime, family violence, and health care expenditures. The federal government estimates that alcohol abuse cost $89.5 billion in 1980 (based on lost production, health costs, accidents, and crime losses).[4] Many of these problems are related to chronic, heavy consumption of alcohol. In a 1979 survey about 2/3 of the American adult population used alcohol, but only 15% of those had experienced problems due to drinking (traffic accidents, family or work problems, alcoholism) in the preceding year.[5] Young people are also drinking in increasing numbers and at an earlier age. Recent studies have shown that 56% of high school seniors had tried alcohol by ninth grade, and 93% had tried by their senior year. Six percent of seniors reported drinking on a daily basis.[6] Drinking and driving has also become the leading cause of death for people aged 16-24.

Increased understanding and awareness of alcohol problems has led to increased involvement by all facets of our society. In addition to research into the causes and most effective treatments for alcohol problems, there has been a recent focus on certain topical issues: alcohol use among special populations (racial and ethnic groups, youth, women, the elderly); the effects of alcohol on the family; legal issues (minimum-age laws, server liability, highway safety legislation); and prevention of alcohol problems. Federal and state agencies, research and academic institutions, school systems, community groups, social service and health care providers have all become concerned with alcohol problems as a public issue.

Scope and Use of the Bibliography

This bibliography is intended for that broad range of persons who are involved with or concerned about alcohol use or alcohol problems in our society. Materials are included for parents, children, teachers, alcohol counselors, social service workers, community groups, and health professionals. Items targeted or especially suited for a particular audience are so described in the annotations; otherwise the audience is assumed to be the general public (senior high school-aged or above). This is not a bibliography for scientific researchers, although several bibliographies that cover research studies have been included (see item nos. 1, 30, and 283). A few additional research studies or overviews have also been included either because of their importance, their accessibility (and readability) to the public, or because information for the public on that particular topic is scarce.

All materials cited in the bibliography are English-language, published materials. Included are books, pamphlets, leaflets, and government documents. Most items are either in print or available in public or academic libraries. Audiovisual materials are not included, but there is a section of published guides to alcohol audiovisuals, and a few curriculum materials that were published for use with audiovisuals are covered. Journal articles are also excluded; however, Appendix A contains a list of periodicals that deal primarily with alcohol problems. Although a few items are dated in the 1960s, the bulk of the entries range from the mid-1970s to 1985, reflecting the recent growth in knowledge and publication about alcohol.

The bibliography is divided into sixteen chapters representing different topical aspects (alcoholism, alcohol problems in the family, alcohol and highway safety, etc.) or formats (general reference and handbooks, audiovisual guides). A scope note at the beginning of each chapter describes the kinds of material to be found in that section. Within each chapter, entries are arranged by author or title, and each includes complete bibliographic information plus a description of content, use, and suitability of the item. Some items are listed by corporate author--either a government agency, professional association, or an institution widely recognized in the alcohol field that issues titles under its own name (for example, the Johnson Institute). Since many items belong under more than one subject heading, there are cross-references at the end of each chapter to lead the user to related items in other sections. In addition, there are author and title indexes as well as a directory of organizations for further information and a list of periodicals dealing with alcohol.

This is a selective bibliography. The purpose is to provide the user with a healthy sampling of the alcohol-related literature currently available. Although I accept responsibility for judging which materials should be included, I also acknowledge my own fallibility and ask the reader to forgive any serious omissions. I hope I have provided enough information to enable the reader to decide which of the materials cited are best suited for his or her use.

References

1. Lender, M.E. and J.K. Martin, DRINKING IN AMERICA: A HISTORY (New York: Free Press, 1982), 196-197.

2. Burnham, J.C., "New Perspectives on the Prohibition 'Experiment' of the 1920s," JOURNAL OF SOCIAL HISTORY 2(1968):51-68.

3. Kinney, J. and G. Leaton, LOOSENING THE GRIP: A HANDBOOK OF ALCOHOL INFORMATION (St. Louis: C.V. Mosby, 1983), 25.

4. Alcohol, Drug Abuse, and Mental Health Administration, ADAMHA DATA BOOK, FY 1983 (Washington, D.C., 1983), 14.

5. National Institute on Alcohol Abuse and Alcoholism, FOURTH SPECIAL REPORT TO THE U.S. CONGRESS ON ALCOHOL AND HEALTH FROM THE SECRETARY OF HEALTH AND HUMAN SERVICES (Washington, D.C.: U.S. Government Printing Office, 1981), 31.

6. ______, FIFTH SPECIAL REPORT TO THE U.S. CONGRESS ON ALCOHOL AND HEALTH FROM THE SECRETARY OF HEALTH AND HUMAN SERVICES (Washington, D.C.: U.S. Government Printing Office, 1984), xiii.

Alcohol Use and Alcoholism

1. GENERAL REFERENCE AND HANDBOOKS

This chapter contains general works on alcohol, its uses, or consequences. Included are overviews, fact books, statistical publications, dictionaries, encyclopedias, bibliographies, and directories of resource organizations. Directories of treatment centers are found in chapter six, **Treatment of Alcoholism.**

1. ALCOHOL BIBLIOGRAPHY SERIES. New Brunswick, N.J.: Rutgers Center of Alcohol Studies, 1980--. approx. 50 pp. each.

Contains separate bibliographical entries on sixty-four different topics relating to alcohol use. The topics cover alcohol use by special populations (blacks, the elderly, women, youth, etc.); various aspects of alcoholism, such as etiology, prevention, and tests for alcoholism; different treatment approaches for alcoholism; medical complications related to alcohol use; and psychological and social aspects of alcohol use, including attitudes toward alcohol use, drinking and driving, and alcohol problems in industry. Each bibliography contains citations to published sources (articles, books, book chapters, government documents, dissertations) as well as some unpublished items, such as conference papers, dating from the 1940s to the present. All bibliographies are updated annually and are available individually. They are suitable for researchers, health or social service professionals, concerned laypersons, and college students. See item 30 for a related series containing some abstracts.

2. Alcohol, Drug Abuse, and Mental Health Administration. ADAMHA DATA BOOK, FISCAL YEAR 1983. 7th ed. Washington, D.C.: U.S. Government Printing Office, 1983. 51 pp.

Summarizes the development and organizational structure of the Alcohol, Drug Abuse, and Mental Health Administration. Presents statistics on alcohol, drug, and mental health problems as well as charts, tables, and graphs on funding levels of research and training in all three major areas. A quick reference for broad statistics on alcohol problems.

3. Andrews, Theodora. A BIBLIOGRAPHY OF DRUG ABUSE, INCLUDING ALCOHOL AND TOBACCO. Littleton, Colo.: Libraries Unlimited, 1977. 306 pp.

Contains decriptions of 725 English-language titles (books, indexes and abstracts, periodicals) on drug use and abuse. The bulk of the materials were published from 1960-1976, and the emphasis is primarily on drugs other than alcohol. Materials are arranged by author in broad categories according to format (e.g., periodicals, reference works) or subject (education and attitudes, drugs and youth, stimulants, etc.). There is a separate section on alcohol with seventy-one entries, and several additional alcohol titles may be found in other sections by using the subject index. An author/title index is also included. Although the book contains materials for all audience levels, the emphasis is on materials for professionals and other interested adult laypersons. No audiovisuals are included.

4. Andrews, Theodora. A BIBLIOGRAPHY OF DRUG ABUSE: SUPPLEMENT 1977-1980. Littleton, Colo.: Libraries Unlimited, 1981. 312 pp.

Updates the original volume of the same title (see item no. 3). Contains 741 annotated entries arranged in the same format as the first volume but includes two new sections on self-help materials and drug use among special population groups (e.g., minorities, women, the elderly) other than youth. The section on alcohol includes forty entries as well as cross-references to several other sections containing alcohol titles. Author/title and subject indexes are provided.

5. Andrews, Theodora. SUBSTANCE ABUSE MATERIALS FOR SCHOOL LIBRARIES: AN ANNOTATED BIBLIOGRAPHY. Littleton, Colo.: Libraries Unlimited, 1985. 215 pp.

Contains descriptions of nearly 500 published materials

dealing with alcohol, tobacco, or other drugs. Inlcudes items suitable for elementary or secondary school-aged children as well as teachers and administrators. Entries are arranged by author within thirteen broad subject or format categories (e.g., periodicals, personal narratives and fiction, drugs and youth). An author/title index and a subject index are provided. Some of the entries were originally included in the author's earlier editions of A BIBLIOGRAPHY OF DRUG ABUSE, INCLUDING ALCOHOL AND TOBACCO (see item nos. 3 and 4).

6. Bemko, Jane. SUBSTANCE ABUSE BOOK REVIEW INDEX Toronto: Addiction Research Foundation, 1978-1979--. approx. 60 pp.

Annual compilation of citations for reviews of books dealing with alcohol or other drug use. Arranged alphabetically by author of book reviewed. Includes title and subject indexes.

7. Block, Marvin A. ALCOHOL AND ALCOHOLISM: DRINKING AND DEPENDENCE. Basic Concepts in Health Science Series. Belmont, Calif.: Wadsworth Publishing Co., 1970. 63 pp.

Surveys several important aspects of alcohol use and abuse. Looks at why people drink, how alcohol affects the body, the symptoms of a drinking problem, and the development and consequences of alcoholism. Also briefly discusses several treatment and prevention approaches for alcohol problems. Includes a short annotated bibliography and a glossary of terms. May be used as a text for college or adult health courses.

8. Chafetz, Morris. WHY DRINKING CAN BE GOOD FOR YOU. New York: Stein and Day, 1976. 191 pp.

Contains basic data about alcohol and its effects, emphasizing the positive aspects of moderate alcohol use. The author corrects a number of popular misconceptions about alcohol use (few women become alcoholics, a drink can cure a hangover, etc.) and presents guidelines for developing safe drinking practices. Also describes the signs of a drinking problem and offers suggestions for getting help. Appendixes describe the effects of various drugs when used with alcohol, the alcohol content of different beverages, and the physiological and behaviorial effects of different blood alcohol levels. There is also a list of state alcoholism authorities and program contacts. Published in reprinted edition under the title HOW DRINKING CAN BE GOOD FOR YOU.

9. Decker, Roberta A., ed. RESOURCE DIRECTORY ON NATIONAL ALCOHOLISM ASSOCIATIONS, AGENCIES AND ORGANIZATIONS. Silver Spring, Md.: Science Management Corp. and Research Studies and Development, 1982. 73 pp.

Describes sixty-seven national organizations primarily concerned with alcohol use or abuse (excluding treatment centers). Items are arranged alphabetically by title of organization. Each entry includes current address and information about purpose, membership, services, and publications. Includes alcoholic beverage industry trade associations, citizens groups, peer-support groups, grant-funding organizations, government agencies, and others, which can be identified via the index based on type of organization.

10. FACTS ABOUT ALCOHOL AND ALCOHOLISM. Pompano Beach, Fla.: Health Communications, 1983. 29 pp.

Presents basic information about alcohol and alcohol use. Includes statistics on alcohol consumption and alcoholism, a blood alcohol concentration chart, and brief descriptions of the short- and long-term effects of alcohol on the body. Identifies several types of treatment programs and approaches and also discusses the impact of alcoholism on the family. A brief discussion of the social costs of alcoholism--such as treatment, accidents, lost productivity on the job--is also included.

11. Forrai, Maria S., and Rebecca Anders. A LOOK AT ALCOHOLISM. Minneapolis: Lerner Publications Co., 1978. 30 pp.

Presents a series of black-and-white photographs with brief accompanying text to introduce elementary school children to the uses and abuses of alcohol. Includes social and religious uses of alcohol, effects of alcohol on the body, and problems caused by alcoholism.

12. Hammond, Robert L. ALMOST ALL YOU EVER WANTED TO KNOW ABOUT ALCOHOL* BUT DIDN'T KNOW WHO TO ASK! Lansing: Michigan Alcohol and Drug Information Foundation, 1978. 64 pp.

Contains information on the history of alcohol use, the manufacture of alcoholic beverages, and the effects of alcohol on the body. Includes statistics on alcohol consumption, alcoholism, drinking and driving, and alcohol-related revenues and expenditures.

13. Hyde, Margaret O. KNOW ABOUT ALCOHOL. New York: McGraw-Hill, 1978. 80 pp.

Presents basic information for children 8-12 years old on alcohol, its use, and misuse. Includes material on the alcoholic content and manufacture of beer, wine, and distilled spirits, as well as the effects of alcohol on the body. Offers suggestions for safe drinking practices and several reasons for not drinking.

14. Hyman. Merton M., Marilyn A. Zimmermann, Carol Gurioli, and Alice Helrich. DRINKERS, DRINKING AND ALCOHOL-RELATED MORTALITY AND HOSPITALIZATIONS: A STATISTICAL COMPENDIUM. New Brunswick, N.J.: Rutgers Center of Alcohol Studies, 1980. 27 pp.

A concise and authoritative source for statistical information on alcohol consumption and alcohol problems. Demographic variables (age, sex, geographic location, income, etc.) are matched with consumption figures and with data on alcohol-related deaths, hospital admissions, and alcoholic beverage control laws. This is the latest in a series which has been published by the Center of Alcohol Studies irregularly since 1952 (under various titles).

15. Keller, Mark, Mairi McCormick, and Vera Efron. A DICTIONARY OF WORDS ABOUT ALCOHOL. 2d ed. New Brunswick, N.J.: Rutgers Center of Alcohol Studies, 1982. 291 pp.

A unique and easy to use reference work containing definitions of over 2,000 words and terms related to alcoholic beverages, alcohol use, and alcohol problems.

Definitions range from a few lines to several pages in length and include origin, meaning, and preferred usage. Proper nouns (such as organizations) and some foreign terms are included.

16. Langone, John. BOMBED, BUZZED, SMASHED, OR...SOBER: A BOOK ABOUT ALCOHOL. Boston: Little, Brown and Co., 1976. 212 pp.

Designed to provide teenagers with basic information about the use and abuse of alcohol. Topics include a brief history of drinking from biblical times through Prohibition, effects of alcohol on the human body, an overview of different treatment modalities, causes of alcoholism, the positive aspects of drinking, and responsible drinking. There is also a glossary of alcoholic beverages and a section on rating one's own drinking habits.

17. Lee, Essie E., and Elaine Israel. ALCOHOL AND YOU. New York: Julian Messner, 1975. 64 pp.

Presents basic information on alcohol and alcohol problems for elementary school readers (grades 3-6). Describes the history of alcohol use in the United States, the effects of alcohol on various body systems, and the long-term effects of alcoholism on individuals and on society (traffic accidents, violence, family problems). The emphasis is on the negative consequences of alcohol abuse. A helpful glossary of terms is included.

18. THE LIQUOR HANDBOOK. New York: Gavin-Jobson Associates, 1953--. approx. 300 pp.

This volume is an annual compilation of statistical data pertaining to consumption, sales, and marketing of distilled spirits in the United States. Includes tables on liquor taxation, liquor production, and storage, as well as a marketing breakdown (covering the top metropolitan sales areas) for the major distilled spirits types. A section on advertising and promotion examines expenditures on various media by the major liquor producers. This is a good source for the most recent consumption and sales figures.

19. Milgram, Gail G. ALCOHOL EDUCATION MATERIALS, AN ANNOTATED BIBLIOGRAPHY. New Brunswick, N.J.: Rutgers Center of Alcohol Studies, 1975. 304 pp.

Contains over 850 bibliographical entries (books, pamphlets, periodicals, curriculum materials) for use by students, educators, alcohol professionals, and interested laypersons. Entries are arranged by author and are indexed by title, audience level, type of publication, and subject categories (such as teenage drinking, alcohol education, and alcoholism treatment). Easy to use and provides helpful, evaluative annotations. Covers literature published between 1950 and mid-1973. A second volume covers 1973-1978 (over 600 items) and also includes a publishers' index.

20. Milgram, Gail G., and Penny B. Page. ALCOHOL EDUCATION MATERIALS, 1978-1979: AN ANNOTATED BIBLIOGRAPHY. Lansing, Mich.: Journal of Alcohol and Drug Education, 1979. 107 pp.

Continuation of title above (no. 19). For three years (1979-1981) this bibliography was published annually as the entire summer issue of the JOURNAL OF ALCOHOL AND DRUG EDUCATION. Format was the same as the earlier volumes, including publishers' index. Over 150 entries in each.

21. Milt, Harry. THE REVISED BASIC HANDBOOK ON ALCOHOLISM. Maplewood, N.J.: Scientific Aids Publications, 1977. 169 pp.

Provides a cohesive overview of alcohol use and alcohol problems. The behavioral and physiological effects of alcohol use are described, as well as the developmental stages of alcoholism. Various theories of alcoholism and contributing factors--both environmental and genetic--are explored, and descriptions of different treatment modalities (drug therapy, behavior therapy, Alcoholics Anonymous, etc.) are included. This book could be successfully used as a college text, an introductory tool for the layman, or a reference manual for the professional in the field.

22. Mitchell, Andrea, ed. THE SALIS DIRECTORY (SUBSTANCE ABUSE LIBRARIANS AND INFORMATION SPECIALISTS) 1984. Berkeley, Calif.: Substance Abuse Librarians and Information Specialists, 1984. 69 pp.

Title includes over 100 libraries, clearinghouses, and information centers involved in collecting and disseminating information on alcohol and other drugs. Entries are arranged alphabetically by geographic location, and each contains address, name of contact person, and descriptions of collections and services offered. Also contains a list of National Alcohol Research Centers, a directory of other associations and organizations concerned with substance abuse (e.g., research institutes, professional or trade associations, advocacy groups), and indexes by organization and by contact person.

23. National Institute on Alcohol Abuse and Alcoholism. ALCOHOL: SOME QUESTIONS AND ANSWERS. Washington, D.C.: U.S. Government Printing Office, 1977. 15 pp.

Answers basic questions about alcoholic beverages and their use. Covers such topics as the alcohol content of various beverages, the effects of alcohol on the body and on behavior, and the risks of heavy drinking.

24. National Institute on Alcohol Abuse and Alcoholism. ALCOHOLISM PREVENTION: GUIDE TO RESOURCES AND REFERENCES. Washington, D.C.: U.S. Government Printing Office, 1979. 88 pp.

Annotated bibliography of materials dealing with primary prevention of alcohol abuse. Entries are arranged by author within broad subject categories such as history, prevention programs, education, evaluation, and media. Includes references to books, journal articles, reports, and conference papers. There is an author index as well as resource lists for audiovisual materials and for further information about alcohol problems.

25. National Institute on Alcohol Abuse and Alcoholism. DRINKING ETIQUETTE: FOR THOSE WHO DRINK AND THOSE WHO DON'T. Washington, D.C.: U.S. Government Printing Office, 1979. 13 pp.

This brief title discusses the different ways in which Americans use alcoholic beverages and offers suggestions for moderate social drinking. Includes tips for giving successful parties without excessive alcohol use.

26. National Institute on Alcohol Abuse and Alcoholism. FIRST STATISTICAL COMPENDIUM ON ALCOHOL AND HEALTH. Washington, D.C.: U.S. Government Printing Office, 1981. 216 pp.

Presents a vast compilation of statistical data relating to alcohol use in the United States. Includes tables on consumption of alcoholic beverages, drinking patterns among various population segments, estimates of numbers of alcoholics, treatment, and funding data. Most figures given are for the 1970s and earlier.

27. O'Brien, Robert, and Morris Chafetz. THE ENCYCLOPEDIA OF ALCOHOLISM. New York: Facts on File Publications, 1982. 378 pp.

Provides information on topics related to alcohol as a substance, alcohol use, alcoholism, and other alcohol-related problems. All of the entries are arranged alphabetically and vary in length from a few lines to several pages. Many contain bibliographies. Includes entries for some temperance groups as well as contemporary organizations devoted to research, treatment, or prevention of alcohol problems, but there are very few entries for individuals. Appendixes contain tables and figures on such topics as age limit for purchase and consumption of alcoholic beverages, alcohol education programs, alcohol funding, alcoholism treatment data, drinking patterns, and economic costs of alcohol abuse. There is also a list of information resources (government agencies, national associations) for the United States and other countries and a selected list of English-language periodicals related to alcohol use. A lengthy bibliography and an index are included.

28. Pace, Nicholas A., with Wilbur Cross. GUIDELINES TO SAFE DRINKING. New York: McGraw-Hill, 1984. 160 pp.

Offers practical guidelines to help moderate drinkers avoid alcohol problems. Identifies the most common settings for consuming alcohol (in the home, at social gatherings, the business lunch, athletic events, etc.) and suggests ways of pacing consumption to avoid intoxication. Also includes a question-and-answer section which covers such topics as pacing drinks, recognizing unsafe drinking habits, and how to get help for alcohol problems.

29. Pursch, Joseph A. DEAR DOC...THE NOTED AUTHORITY ANSWERS YOUR QUESTIONS ON DRINKING AND DRUGS. Minneapolis: CompCare Publications, 1985. 327 pp.

Presents information and advice on alcohol and other drug use. Discusses how and why Americans use alcohol and drugs, focusing on such settings as athletics and the workplace. Includes a chapter aimed primarily at physicians to help them identify and deal with alcohol-related problems. Also discusses the effects of addiction on family members and offers suggestions for coping with problems experienced during recovery.

30. RECENT TOPICS IN ALCOHOL STUDIES. New Brunswick, N.J.: Rutgers Center of Alcohol StudIes, 1980--. approx. 100 pp. each.

Companion to the ALCOHOL BIBLIOGRAPHY SERIES (see no. 1) covering a number of topics not included in that group. There are forty-four separate bibliographies, each covering a different topic on alcohol use. Most topics deal with the medical complications of alcohol use (liver disease, cardiovascular problems, etc.), physiological or biochemical effects of alcohol (with separate bibliographies for each of the body systems), or psychological aspects of alcohol use (cognitive functions, personality aspects, polydrug addiction, and psychomotor functions). However, there are also several bibliographies that deal with alcoholic beverages (properties, manufacturing), alcohol-related mortality, drinking experiments, detoxification and treatment of withdrawal, and drug therapies. In addition, there are a few topics related to social aspects of alcohol use (economic, legal, and safety aspects) outside the United States. These bibliographies were originally compiled in 1980 for a professional or research audience, and they cite literature only as far back as 1977. Entries through 1980 include abstracts and cover all types of published (and some unpublished) print materials. Since 1983 the series has been updated annually with citations only. Individual bibliographies are available separately.

31. Sexias, Judith S. ALCOHOL--WHAT IT IS, WHAT IT DOES. New York: Greenwillow Books, 1977. 56 pp.

Title presents basic information for elementary school students about alcoholic beverages and their effects on the body. There is also a section which stresses the concept that alcoholism is a sickness. The text is illustrated and concludes with a helpful list of common beliefs about alcohol and its use.

32. United States Brewers Association. BREWERS ALMANAC: THE BREWING INDUSTRY IN THE UNITED STATES. Washington, D.C.: United States Brewers Association, 1940 --. 100 pp.

Annual Compilation of statistical data on the brewing industry (beer and other malt beverages). Tables cover production, consumption, taxation, sales, exports, and imports for the United States. There is also a helpful section outlining existing local option and state beverage control laws.

33. United States Jaycees, Operation Threshold. DRINKING MYTHS: A GUIDED TOUR THROUGH FOLKLORE, FANTASY AND HOGWASH. Tulsa, Okla.: United States Jaycees, 1975. 22 pp.

Title uses cartoon illustrations to correct a number of popular misconceptions about alcohol use (e.g., "Most alcoholics are Skid Row bums"; "I drive better after a few drinks"). Includes information on the effects of alcohol on behavior and on driving ability.

34. United States Jaycees, Operation Threshold. SOCIAL DRINKING: FOR PEOPLE WHO DRINK AND PEOPLE WHO DON'T. Tulsa, Okla.: United States Jaycees, 1975. 16 pp.

Identifies most of the common characteristics of social (non-problem) drinking and offers suggestions for hosts and hostesses to discourage excessive alcohol use at social gatherings. Explains the relationship between alcohol use and driving ability and includes a brief self-test to discover possible alcohol problems.

35. WHAT EVERY KID SHOULD KNOW ABOUT ALCOHOL. South Deerfield, Mass.: Channing L. Bete Co., 1982. 15 pp.

Explains how alcohol affects the body and behavior and describes the signs of problem drinking and alcoholism.

Discusses why alcohol can be dangerous for young people and corrects some common myths and misinformation about alcohol use.

36. WHAT EVERYONE SHOULD KNOW ABOUT ALCOHOL. South Deerfield, Mass.: Channing L. Bete Co., 1973. 15 pp.

Illustrates basic information about alcohol, including the alcoholic context of beverages, the stages of intoxication, and reasons why people use alcohol. Includes a section on the consequences of alcohol abuse, such as traffic accidents, sickness, violence, and lost productivity in the workplace. Describes the common signs of alcoholism and its adverse effects on the body.

37. THE WINE MARKETING HANDBOOK. New York: Gavin-Jobson Associates, 1971--. approx. 150 pp.

Source presents current statistical information on wine sales, consumption, taxation, exports, and imports for the United States. Includes marketing statistics for each of the major wine types--table wine, dessert wine, champagne and sparkling wine, and vermouth. The section on wine advertising breaks down expenditures by type of media and wine producer or importer. There is also a helpful section on malt beverages that includes advertising, revenue, and consumption figures. Published annually.

See also: 38, 43, 51, 89, 240, 361, 368, 369, 383.

2. AUDIOVISUAL GUIDES

Published guides that list or describe non-print materials (films, cassettes, videotapes, slides, sound recordings) on alcohol use are cited in this chapter. Most of the guides provide some type of description or evaluation as well as prices and distributors' addresses.

38. EDUCATION-FOR-HEALTH, THE SELECTIVE GUIDE: HEALTH PROMOTION, FAMILY LIFE, AND MENTAL HEALTH AUDIOVISUALS AND PUBLICATIONS. New York: National Center for Health Education, 1983. 927 pp.

Provides an annotated listing of print and audiovisual materials dealing with a variety of mental health topics. Part one contains audiovisual titles arranged in nine sections (awareness-for-health, human growth and development, environmental health, etc.) that are further broken down into subject categories. The section on alcohol and alcoholism contains nearly fifty entries listed alphabetically by title. Each entry includes descriptive details, sale and rental information, synopsis and evaluation of content and presentation, and an audience guide. In part two publications (pamphlets, books, and government documents) are similarly arranged and provide full publication details (including price and publisher's address). There are fifty-five entries for alcoholism. Subject and title indexes for publications and audiovisuals are included, but there is no author index.

39. Kinsolving, Janice, and Craig Wunderlich. PROJECTING: A FACILITATOR'S GUIDE TO ALCOHOL AND OTHER DRUG FILM UTILIZATION. Madison: Wisconsin Clearinghouse, 1979. 56 pp.

Provides guidelines for planning and presenting a program on alcohol or drugs using film as an aide. Discusses how to use films most effectively in a program, how to select films, how to set up a film presentation, how to lead film discussions, how to handle problems that may arise from film showings or group discussions, and how to conduct an evaluation of the overall program. Although this booklet does not list or describe any films, it does include a list of published guides that do describe or evaluate alcohol and drug films, a list of books for group facilitators, and a brief list of titles on operating audiovisual equipment. This booklet would be a very useful tool for educators, community workers, and social service personnel.

40. National Institute on Alcohol Abuse and Alcoholism. IN FOCUS: ALCOHOL AND ALCOHOLISM AUDIOVISUAL GUIDE. rev. ed. Washington, D.C.: U.S. Government Printing Office, 1980. 86 pp.

Lists and describes audiovisual materials dealing with alcohol use and abuse. Entries are arranged alphabetically by title and include sale and rental information. A subject area index is provided. Also includes a list of publications dealing with media resources and a list of organizations for information about alcohol problems.

41. National Library of Medicine. NATIONAL LIBRARY OF MEDICINE AUDIOVISUALS CATALOG. Washington, D.C.: U.S. Government Printing Office, 1978--. approx. 100 pp.

Lists and describes current audiovisual materials received and cataloged by the National Library of Medicine. Entries are arranged by name (author or creator) and title and also by subject headings (in a separate section). Each entry in the name and title section provides descriptive information, sale and rental prices, the procurement source for obtaining the item, medical subject headings, and National Library of Medicine cataloging information. Some entries also include abstracts, review information, and audience level. The procurement section contains addresses for all the distributors listed in the entries. There is also an audiovisual serials index that cites selected audiocassette and videocassette serials currently being indexed by the National Library of Medicine. Items dealing with alcohol use or alcohol problems can be located in the catalog by author or title (if known) or by using the appropriate medical subject headings (alcohol, drinking, alcoholic beverages, alcoholism, etc.) as found in INDEX

MEDICUS or in separately published guides and thesauri compiled by the National Library of Medicine. The catalog is published quarterly, including an annual cumulation.

42. PCR: FILMS AND VIDEO IN THE BEHAVIORAL SCIENCES. University Park, Pa.: The Pennsylvania State University, 1944--. approx. 200 pp.

Lists and briefly describes audiovisuals in the behavioral sciences, including such areas as alcohol and drug abuse, adolescence, aging, bahavior modification, counseling, ethnography, mental health, psycopathology, sexuality, therapy, and women. Items are listed alphabetically by title and are available for rent or sale from PCR. A subject index and an author-advisor index are included. Published biennially since 1944.

43. RESOURCE REVIEWS: FILM AND LITERATURE EVALUATIONS. ALCOHOL AND OTHER DRUGS, 1979-1983. Madison: Wisconsin Clearinghouse, 1984. 272 pp.

Contains concise reviews of audiovisuals, pamphlets, books, curricula, and other resources on alcohol and drugs reprinted from CRITIQUES (no longer published). Each review provides title, author, publisher or distributor, cost, subject area, synopsis, evaluation, and recommendations for use. There are no indexes.

3. HISTORY OF ALCOHOL USE AND MISUSE

Historical accounts of American drinking practices, attitudes toward alcohol use, and approaches to alcohol problems will be found in this section. Also included are biographies of leaders in the Temperance and Prohibition Movements as well as contemporary figures known for their involvement with treatment or prevention of alcohol problems.

44. Alcoholics Anonymous. DR. BOB AND THE GOOD OLD-TIMERS: A BIOGRAPHY, WITH RECOLLECTIONS OF EARLY A.A. IN THE MIDWEST. New York: Alcoholics Anonymous World Services, 1980. 373 pp.

Describes the life of Dr. Bob Smith, one of the co-founders of Alcoholics Anonymous. Depicts the early development of A.A. with emphasis on the contributions of the Oxford Group and the Cleveland and Akron, Ohio, A.A. groups. Based on A.A. archives and interviews with early A.A. members.

45. Alcoholics Anonymous. "PASS IT ON": THE STORY OF BILL WILSON AND HOW THE A.A. MESSAGE REACHED THE WORLD. New York: Alcoholics Anonymous World Services, 1984. 429 pp.

Biography of Bill Wilson, co-founder of Alcoholics Anonymous (A.A.), based primarily on material in A.A. archives. Describes his childhood family ties, marriage, career on Wall Street, onset and progression of drinking, and the spiritual experience that began his recovery from alcoholism. Details his experiences with the Oxford Group, his meeting with Dr. Bob Smith, and their successful efforts to establish a fellowship for alcoholics. Includes photographs and such interesting revelations as Bill's communication with the "world beyond" and his experimentation with LSD. Contains index and references (to published sources only).

46. Clark, Norman H. DELIVER US FROM EVIL: AN INTERPRETATION OF AMERICAN PROHIBITION. New York: W.W. Norton and Co., 1976. 246 pp.

Explores the diverse origins and development of the American Temperance Movement from colonial times through the repeal of National Prohibition. Examines the impact of temperance efforts on the political, intellectual, and social history of the nation. Also demonstrates a strong relationship between National Prohibition and popular concerns over the status of the family in America. This book should be especially useful for historians, college or senior high school students, or others interested in American social history or the Temperance Movement. Includes a list of source materials and index.

47. Coffey, Thomas W. THE LONG THIRST, 1920-1933. New York: W.W. Norton and Co., 1975. 346 pp.

Identifies the factors which ultimately led to the repeal of Prohibition in 1933, focusing in particular on the actions of major personalities during the Prohibition years. Discusses the leadership of the Anti-Saloon League, government and enforcement officials, and prominent wets such as Al Smith. Also includes many of the most notorious criminals who profited from the illegal liquor trade.

48. Earhart, Mary. FRANCES WILLARD: FROM PRAYERS TO POLITICS. Chicago: University of Chicago Press, [1944]. 417 pp.

Chronicles the life of Frances Willard, well known for her role in the Temperance Movement and her leadership of the Woman's Christian Temperance Union in the latter part of the nineteenth century. Describes her family background, education, teaching career, and long-term interest in the issues of temperance, woman's suffrage, labor, and welfare.

49. Fleming, Alice. ALCOHOL: THE DELIGHTFUL POISON. New York: Dell Publishing Co., 1975. 138 pp.

Presents a brief history of alcohol use and abuse. Covers the production and use of alcoholic beverages in ancient societies in Egypt, the Middle East, and Europe; also includes a section on the origin of alcohol-related terms in the English language. Chronicles alcohol use in the United States from colonial times through Prohibition, focusing in particular on national policies and legislation regarding the control of alcoholic beverages. Concludes with a section on attitudes and treatment regarding alcoholism throughout history as well as the effects of alcohol on the body. Includes photographs and other illustrations.

50. Kurtz, Ernest. NOT-GOD: A HISTORY OF ALCOHOLICS ANONYMOUS. Center City, Minn.: Hazelden, 1979. 363pp.

Describes the development of Alcoholics Anonymous both as fellowship and program. Details the history of A.A. including persons and groups that influenced its founding, growth, and change over the years. Also presents an interpretation of A.A. philosophy, placing it within the larger contexts of American historical development and the history of religious ideas reflected in the program. There are an extensive reference list, an annotated bibliography, and indexes. The book provides valuable knowledge and insights for the scholar as well as the interested layperson.

51. Lender, Mark E. DICTIONARY OF AMERICAN TEMPERANCE BIOGRAPHY: FROM TEMPERANCE REFORM TO ALCOHOL RESEARCH, THE 1600S TO THE 1980S. Westport, Conn.: Greenwood Press, 1984. 572 pp.

Provides biographical information for 373 individuals who were active in the Temperance Movement or other efforts to deal with alcohol problems in the United States. Also includes several prominent members of the modern alcohol research movement. Entries are arranged alphabetically and each includes dates and places of birth and death, educational data, narrative information about careers and activities related to alcohol reform or research, a list of the individual's most important writings, and a list of secondary sources for more information. There is a general index as well as a listing by birthplace and a listing by religious affiliation. This is a particularly valuable sourcebook for scholars and students.

52. Lender, Mark E., and Karen R. Karnchanapee. TEMPERANCE TALES AND THE ALCOHOLIC: CREATION OF A STEREOTYPE, 1850-1930. New Brunswick, N.J.: Rutgers Center of

Alcohol Studies, 1979. 16 pp. plus 113 slides and 1 audiocassette.

Versatile and informative educational tool that deals with American practices and attitudes in the past regarding alcohol. Focuses in particular on the activities of temperance groups and on the creation of the "Skid Row" stereotype of the alcoholic. Complete set includes 113 slides, accompanying sound track, and leader's guide that explains how to use the program and contains an annotated script describing the slides. May be used in classrooms or with civic groups to focus on issues involving history, sociology, public health, or literature.

53. Lender, Mark E., and James K. Martin. DRINKING IN AMERICA: A HISTORY. New York: The Free Press, 1982. 222 pp.

Examines drinking and alcohol use in the United States from colonial times to the present. Describes drinking practices (prevalence of alcohol use, beverage preferences, reasons for alcohol use) of the various social, ethnic, and cultural groups that have comprised American society. Also discusses the development of American attitudes toward alcohol use and drunkenness and looks at the variety of approaches that have been used to prevent or deal with alcohol problems (the Temperance Movement, Prohibition and other legal controls, treatment, alcohol education). Contains a large number of excellent illustrations (copies of paintings, engravings, photographs, temperance posters, etc.). There is also an appendix with alcohol consumption figures from 1790-1978, a detailed list of source materials, and an index. This book is well documented and also highly readable; it would be suitable for scholars, educators, college students, or the general public.

54. Rorabaugh, W.J. THE ALCOHOLIC REPUBLIC: AN AMERICAN TRADITION. New York: Oxford University Press, 1979. 302 pp.

Surveys American drinking practices during the first fifty years of the new nation (1790-1840). Discusses where, how, and why Americans drank alcohol as well as how much and which alcoholic beverages they preferred. Also explores several theories as to why alcohol consumption increased dramatically in the early years of the republic and how consumption was affected by the rise of the American Temperance Movement. Appendixes include estimates of alcohol consumption from 1710-1975, cross-national comparisons of consumption for the U.S. and various European countries, and a discussion of the use of quantitative measurements in historical research. Includes extensive references plus index. Useful for historians or other social researchers, college students, or others interested in American social history or the origins of the Temperance Movement.

55. Smithers, Christopher D., Foundation. PIONEERS WE HAVE KNOWN IN THE FIELD OF ALCOHOLISM. Mill Neck, N.Y.: Christopher D. Smithers Foundation, 1979. 216 pp.

Contains short biographies of nearly 100 persons who have been involved in research, treatment, or information about alcohol use and alcohol problems. The entries come from all parts of the world, and most were still living at the time of this publication. Each biography describes the individual's background and contributions to the area of alcohol problems or research. In addition there is a brief history of some of the important modern (post 1930) organizations concerned with alcohol and its use, such as Alcoholics Anonymous, the Yale (later Rutgers) Center of Alcohol Studies, the National Council on Alcoholism, and the Christopher D. Smithers Foundation. There are photographs for most entries.

56. Thomsen, Robert. BILL W. New York: Harper and Row, 1975. 373 pp.

Comprehensive biography of Bill Wilson, co-founder of Alcoholics Anonymous. Describes his childhood, his career, the onset and progression of his alcoholism, his recovery, and the struggles involved with the founding and early years of Alcoholics Anonymous.

See also: 17, 66, 67, 96, 129, 383.

4. EFFECTS OF ALCOHOL ON THE BODY

The materials in this chapter look at the effects of alcohol use on body systems and functions as well as on behavior and emotions. Items dealing with the interactions between alcohol and other drugs are also included.

57. ALCOHOL AND DRUG COMBINATIONS: WHEN 1+1 DOESN'T EQUAL 2. Pompano Beach, Fla.: Health Communications, 1983. 12 pp.

Briefly describes the risks involved in using alcohol with other drugs such as marijuana, amphetamines, tranquilizers, and sedative-hypnotics. Focuses on behavioral and physiological consequences, stressing the danger of potentiating (increased) effects when drugs are used together (over and above their effects when used individually).

58. Center for Science in the Public Interest. CHEMICAL ADDITIVES IN BOOZE. Washington, D.C.: Center for Science in the Public Interest, 1982. 133 pp.

Reference source identifies a variety of chemicals used in the production of beer, wine, and distilled spirits that can have negative health consequences to consumers. Also looks at the campaign started in 1972 by the Center for Science in the Public Interest to require the alcohol beverage industry to put ingredient labels on all alcoholic beverages. Appendixes include lists of ingredients for some of the most popular alcoholic beverages, calorie and alcohol content of alcoholic beverages (by brand name), and corporate profiles of the major brewers, wine companies, and distillers in the United States.

59. Cohen, Sidney, and Phyllis J. Lessin. MARIJUANA AND ALCOHOL. Rockville, Md.: American Council on

Marijuana and Other Psychoactive Drugs, 1982. 28 pp.

Title summarizes research studies on the various physiological and behavioral effects of combined marijuana and alcohol use, including the effects on driving ability. Contains a glossary of terms and a table comparing the actions of alcohol and marijuana.

60. DO YOU KNOW THE FACTS ABOUT DRUGS? A GUIDE OF DRUG INFORMATION. Pompano Beach, Fla.: Health Communications, 1983. 47 pp.

Provides basic information about the use and abuse of the most common psychoactive (mood-altering) drugs, including alcohol, amphetamines, barbiturates, cannabis, cocaine, hallucinogens, narcotics, and tranquilizers. Briefly describes the effects of alcohol on the human body and the consequences of long-term abuse. Also includes statistics on alcohol consumption patterns in the United States.

61. Geller, Anne. ALCOHOL AND ANXIETY. Minneapolis: Johnson Institute, 1983. 27 pp.

Discusses normal and abnormal anxiety and their relationship to alcohol use. Examines the role of anxiety in the development of physical and psychological dependence on alcohol and offers brief suggestions to physicians in dealing with patients who exhibit anxiety disorders.

62. Geller, Anne. ALCOHOL AND SEXUAL PERFORMANCE. Minneapolis: Johnson Institute, 1984. 22 pp.

Describes the physiological and psychological effects of alcohol use on sexual desire and performance. Includes brief discussions of alcoholism and sexual function, sexual deviance, and sexual behavior during recovery from alcoholism.

63. Gust, Dodie. UP: DOWN: AND SIDEWAYS ON WET AND DRY BOOZE. Minneapolis: CompCare Publications, 1977. 23 pp.

Describes the mood-altering effects of a variety of

drugs that act on the central nervous system, including alcohol, tranquilizers, and amphetamines. Also discusses the dangers of interaction from multiple drug use.

64. Hazelden Foundation. LEARN ABOUT ALCOHOL. Hazelden Learning Series. Center City, Minn.: Hazelden, 1983. 15 pp.

Briefly outlines some basic facts about the effects of alcohol on the body and on behavior. Includes such topics as absorption and metabolism of alcohol, blood alcohol concentration, nutritional value of alcohol, costs (economic and social) of alcohol abuse, and alcoholism. Suitable for junior high or high school students.

65. Keller, Mark. HOW ALCOHOL AFFECTS THE BODY. Popular Pamphlets on Alcohol Problems, no. 3. New Brunswick, N.J.: Rutgers Center of Alcohol Studies, 1972. 16 pp.

Offers concise, factual information on how alcohol is metabolized and how it affects various parts of the body, including the brain, stomach, kidneys, liver, glands, heart, eyes, and ears. Describes the process of intoxication and the effects of various blood alcohol levels on the brain.

66. Milgram, Gail G. COPING WITH ALCOHOL. New York: Richards Rosen Press, 1980. 108 pp.

Provides information for adolescents to help clarify their understanding and attitudes toward alcoholism. Most of the book is written in question-and-answer format covering such topics as the history of alcohol use, how alcoholic beverages are made, the effects of alcohol on the body, the disease and treatment of alcoholism, and drinking patterns and behaviors. Also included is a discussion of alcoholism as a family illness and some sample values clarification exercises. There is a helpful bibliography, a list of information sources, and a glossary of terms. The book is nonjudgmental and easy to read; it could also be helpful for parents and educators.

67. Milgram, Gail G. WHAT IS ALCOHOL? AND WHY DO PEOPLE DRINK? 2d ed. New Brunswick, N.J.: Rutgers Center of Alcohol Studies, 1976. 13 pp.

A brief but well-written introduction to the nature of alcoholic beverages and their use. Includes a helpful explanation and chart of blood alcohol concentrations.

68. Nebraska. Division on Alcoholism and Drug Abuse. NUTRITION AND ALCOHOL. Alcohol Effects Series. Lincoln: Nebraska Alcohol and Drug Information Clearinghouse, n.d. 3 pp.

Leaflet summarizes the effects of alcohol on nutrition. Describes the consequences of substituting alcohol for food, including the negative effects on absorption of important nutrients.

69. Premer, Robert F. MEDICAL CONSEQUENCES OF ALCOHOLISM. Minneapolis: Johnson Institute, 1982. 19 pp.

Briefly outlines the effects of alcohol on the major organs of the body--heart, liver, brain, gastrointestinal tract. Includes a description of how alcohol is absorbed and metabolized in the body and also identifies the risks of alcohol and drug interactions, fetal alcohol syndrome, and alcoholism.

70. Van Almen, William J. 500 DRUGS THE ALCOHOLIC SHOULD AVOID. Center City, Minn.: Hazelden, 1983. 35 pp.

Lists common prescription and over-the-counter drugs that contain alcohol. Provides trade name, alcohol content, and manufacturer for each drug. Also includes a listing of drugs that may interact with alcohol. Especially helpful for abstaining alcoholics.

71. WHAT EVERYONE SHOULD KNOW ABOUT ALCOHOL AND HEALTH. South Deerfield, Mass.: Channing L. Bete Co., 1984. 15 pp.

Briefly identifies the effects of alcohol on the body and on behavior. Focuses on the negative consequences of prolonged heavy alcohol use, including alcoholism, liver damage, heart disease, and alcohol-related birth defects.

See also: 10, 17, 21, 31, 77, 96, 401.

5. ALCOHOLISM

Materials that focus primarily on the physical or psychological addiction to alcohol are included in this chapter. Entries cover the causes of alcoholism as well as the warning signs and long-term consequences. There are materials for professionals (therapists, social workers, health care providers) as well as for the general public. For items on the treatment of alcoholism, see chapter six.

72. Bissell, LeClair, and Richard Watherwax. THE CAT WHO DRANK TOO MUCH. Bantum, Conn.: The Bibulophile Press, 1982. 24 pp.

Photographic tale with brief captions about the development and progression of alcoholism. Includes a short list of sources for help and information. Suitable for use with elementary school-aged children.

73. Blume, Sheila B. ALCOHOLISM AND DEPRESSION. Minneapolis: Johnson Institute, 1984. 31 pp.

Discusses the various meanings of depression (as a mood state, as a symptom, as a diagnosis of mental disorder) and describes the common forms of clinical depression. Examines the relationship between depression and alcoholism, looking both at depression as a contributing factor and as a result of alcoholism. Includes guidelines to help medical and treatment personnel diagnose and treat depression in alcoholics.

74. Blume, Sheila B. THE DISEASE CONCEPT OF ALCOHOLISM TODAY. Minneapolis: Johnson Institute, 1983. 36 pp.

Booklet examines the definition of alcoholism as a disease, including the historical background of the concept and its present use. Outlines the pros and cons of the concept and discusses some recent moral, legal, political, and theoretical objections to its use.

75. Cohen, Sidney. THE ALCOHOLISM PROBLEMS: SELECTED ISSUES. New York: The Haworth Press, 1983. 193 pp.

Presents information on causes and consequences of a variety of alcohol-related problems. The text is divided into three parts: problems caused by the substance alcohol (such as fetal alcohol syndrome, alcoholic hypoglycemia, liver disease); problems related to alcoholism (blackouts, withdrawal, problems among special population groups); and problems and interactions of alcohol with other drugs. Useful for professionals or laypersons interested in alcohol problems.

76. Duren, Ryne, with Robert Drury. THE COMEBACK. Dayton, Ohio: Lorenz Press, 1978. 169 pp.

Tells the story of major league baseball pitcher Ryne Duren, whose career and marriage were destroyed through his alcoholism. Describes the factors which led to his alcohol problems, focusing particularly on the association between alcohol use and professional sports. Includes photographs of Duren and several well-known baseball personalities.

77. Estes, Nada J., and M. Edith Heinemann. ALCOHOLISM: DEVELOPMENT, CONSEQUENCES, AND INTERVENTIONS. 2d ed. St. Louis: C.V. Mosby Co., 1982. 385 pp.

Provides major source of theoretical information about alcoholism and related problems for counselors, health care professionals, and others working with clients who have alcohol problems. Part I deals with the etiology and epidemiology (cause and spread) of alcoholism, including criteria for diagnosis. Part II describes the negative consequences of alcohol abuse on various body systems. Part III focuses on alcohol use among specific populations, such as teenagers, children of alcoholics, women, and Indians, and also includes a chapter on fetal alcohol syndrome. Part IV highlights a variety of treatment approaches for alcohol abuse, including counseling, Alcoholics Anonymous, and behavioral approaches. Although written for professionals, this book could be useful for laypersons interested in theories of development or treatment of alcohol problems.

78. Freed, Earl X. AN ALCOHOLIC PERSONALITY? Thorofare, N.J.: Charles B. Slack, 1979. 97 pp.

Describes research, both for and against, on the existence of an alcoholic personality. Explores a variety of related issues such as cause and effect relationships between alcoholism and personality, conceptualizations of alcoholism, the link between conflict and alcohol use, and depression as a factor in alcoholism.

79. Goodwin, Donald W. ALCOHOLISM: THE FACTS. New York: Oxford University Press, 1981. 135 pp.

Offers concise, accurate information on alcohol, alcohol use, and alcoholism. Describes the effects of alcohol on the body, the symptoms and progression of alcoholism, and various treatment approaches. Also examines such aspects as the relationship between alcoholism and depression and the possible link between alcoholism and heredity.

80. Goodwin, Donald. IS ALCOHOLISM HEREDITARY? New York: Oxford University Press, 1976. 171 pp.

Study examines the relationships between heredity, environment, and alcoholism. Begins with basic information about alcohol and its effects on the body and discusses alcoholism in terms of medical, psychological, and social consequences. Presents research evidence on both sides of the nature (heredity) vs. nurture (environment) issue in the development of alcoholism.

81. Gust, Dodie. DRUNK JOKES ARE FUNNY, BUT.... Minneapolis: CompCare Publications, 1977. 15 pp.

Short title explores the serious side of problem drinking including reasons behind excessive alcohol use, hangovers, blackouts, impaired driving skills, and denial of an alcohol problem. Corrects some common misconceptions about alcohol use while focusing attention on contemporary attitudes toward alcohol use and alcohol-related problems.

82. Harrison, Earl. BOOZLEBANE ON ALCOHOLISM. Center City, Minn.: Hazelden, 1984. 12 pp.

Booklet offers a tongue-in-cheek "lecture" on the most common characteristics of alcoholics and the disease of alcoholism. Identifies many popular misconceptions such as the idea that most alcoholics are Skid Row bums. Briefly describes the Alcoholics Anonymous program and its emphasis on the spiritual dimension of alcoholism.

83. Hatsukami, Dorothy, and Roy Pickens. DEPRESSION AND ALCOHOLISM. Center City, Minn.: Hazelden, 1980. 20 pp.

Provides overview of research on the relationship between alcoholism and depression and distinguishes between primary and secondary depression. Identifies sources of depression in alcoholics and offers suggestions for diagnosing and treating depressed alcoholics.

84. Hazelden Foundation. DEALING WITH DENIAL. Center City, Minn.: Hazelden, 1975. 32 pp.

Briefly describes the process of denial in alcoholism, including its origins, its manifestations, and how it perpetuates the disease of alcoholism. Offers practical suggestions to help counselors, social workers, or other social service caregivers confront the alcoholic and break through the denial system in order to gain recovery.

85. Heilman, Richard O. EARLY RECOGNITION OF ALCOHOLISM AND OTHER DRUG DEPENDENCE. Center City, Minn.: Hazelden, 1977. 12 pp.

Describes the symptoms of alcoholic drinking which are often present in the early stages of the disease of alcoholism. These symptoms represent a pattern of nonsocial drinking that focuses on the desire to "get high."

86. Jellinek, E.M. THE DISEASE CONCEPT OF ALCOHOLISM. New Haven, Conn.: Hillhouse Press, 1960. 246 pp.

Traces the development of the disease theory of alcoholism and discusses the major components (loss of control, inability to abstain, craving and compulsion, tolerance and habituation). Critiques the major research on the etiological theories of alcoholism, including psychological, physiological, nutritional, and pharmacological approaches. Also discusses the role of social, cultural, and economic factors in alcohol addiction and includes an analysis of a survey of attitudes around the world toward a disease conception of alcoholism. Proposes a disease model with five species of alcoholism distinguished by different patterns and effects of alcohol use. This book is responsible for much of the current widespread acceptance of alcoholism as a disease.

87. Johnson Institute. MAKING CHOICES: HOW ALCOHOL AND OTHER DRUGS CAN AFFECT YOUR LIFE. Minneapolis: Johnson Institute, 1981. 21 pp.

Designed to provide information about alcohol and drug addiction for economically and socially stable adults who use alcohol or other drugs. Describes the symptoms of addiction and discusses the problems--family, job, legal, physical--that can result from alcoholism or drug abuse.

88. Jones, Penny. THE BROWN BOTTLE. Center City, Minn.: Hazelden, 1983. 35 pp.

Presents the allegorical tale of a caterpillar who gives up his hopes and dreams when he falls under the influence of alcohol. May be used as a prevention tool for children or a therapeutic tool for breaking denial patterns in alcoholics. Includes illustrations.

89. Kinney, Jean, and Gwen Leaton. LOOSENING THE GRIP: A HANDBOOK OF ALCOHOL INFORMATION. 2d ed. St. Louis: C.V. Mosby, 1983. 353 pp.

A well-written, easy-to-use manual on alcohol problems and their treatment. Examines the scope and etiology of alcohol problems, effects of alcohol on the body, medical complications, behavioral and family problems, psychiatric disorders, and alcohol use among special populations (women, the elderly, adolescents, and the unemployed). There is a lengthy section on treatment which breaks down into a variety of approaches, including group therapy, family therapy, Alcoholics Anonymous, and behavior therapy. Also included is a helpful discussion of professional issues in the alcohol counseling field. The text is suitable for laypersons and has also been successfully used for training alcohol professionals.

90. Luks, Allan, ed. HAVING BEEN THERE. New York: Charles Scribner's Sons, 1979. 189 pp.

Informative presentation of eighteen short stories depicting the experiences of alcoholics at various stages of their disease and recovery. Also includes several stories showing the effects of alcoholism on other family members and close friends. Introduced by Ring Lardner, Jr.

91. McFarland, Barbara. SEXUALITY AND RECOVERY. Center City, Minn.: Hazelden, 1984. 19 pp.

Describes the effects of alcoholism on sexuality and discusses the need for sexual growth and understanding during alcoholism recovery. Presents guidelines for clarifying sex roles and reestablishing healthy sexual relationships.

92. Mann, Marty. MARTY MANN ANSWERS YOUR QUESTIONS ABOUT DRINKING AND ALCOHOLISM. New York: Holt, Rinehart and Winston, 1981. 113 pp.

Answers the most frequently-asked questions about alcohol use and provides statistics on alcohol consumption and alcohol-related problems. Describes the symptoms and possible causes of alcoholism and briefly outlines a variety of treatment approaches. Separate sections are included on Alcoholics Anonymous and on Al-Anon and Alateen (for concerned families and friends).

93. Milam, James R. THE EMERGENT COMPREHENSIVE CONCEPT OF ALCOHOLISM. rev. ed. Kirkland, Wash.: Alcoholism Center Associates, 1974. 70 pp.

Presents a model of alcoholism based on physiological susceptibility to alcohol. Argues that psychosocial problems are important, but secondary, in the development of alcoholism, and demonstrates the difficulties that are caused by physiological changes during and after withdrawal from alcohol. Suggests a multifaceted treatment approach involving physiological recovery, alcohol education and counseling regarding the nature of alcoholism and recovery. Designed for physicians and other alcohol treatment personnel.

94. Milam, James R., and Katherine Ketcham. UNDER THE INFLUENCE: A GUIDE TO THE MYTHS AND REALITIES OF ALCOHOLISM. Seattle: Madrona Publishers, 1981. 210 pp.

Title presents evidence to support the theory that alcoholism is primarily a physiological disease based on individual susceptibility to alcohol. Describes the stimulant and sedative effects of alcohol and identifies several predisposing factors toward alcoholism, such as abnormal metabolism, hereditary influences, and ethnic susceptibilities to alcohol. Discusses the progressive stages of alcoholism and offers sugggestions for motivating the alcoholic into treatment. Outlines a model treatment program based on physiological recovery, nutritional discipline, understanding the nature of alcoholism, and participation in Alcoholics Anonymous. Appendixes include nutritional guidelines plus a list of medications containing alcohol. Written for alcoholics or persons involved in their treatment.

95. National Institute on Alcohol Abuse and Alcoholism. FACING UP TO ALCOHOLISM. Washington, D.C.: U.S. Government Printing Office, 1981. 11 pp.

Presents a brief, concise description of the symptoms of alcoholism and offers practical suggestions for selecting a treatment approach for the alcoholic and his or her family members. Includes a short list of sources for help or referral.

96. National Institute on Alcohol Abuse and Alcoholism. FACTS ABOUT ALCOHOL AND ALCOHOLISM. Prepared by Leonard C. Hall. Washington, D.C.: U.S. Government Printing Office, 1974. 44 pp.

A handy, quick reference on alcoholic beverages, alcohol use, and alcohol problems. Includes the physiological and behavioral effects of alcohol use, some factors contributing to alcohol problems, and a breakdown of the diagnosis and treatment approaches for alcoholism. There is also a helpful section describing various sources of information and help for alcohol problems.

97. Nebraska. Division on Alcoholism and Drug Abuse. ALCOHOLISM IN OUR SOCIETY. Lincoln: Nebraska Alcohol and Drug Information Clearinghouse, 1980. 10 pp.

Brief title provides a concise reference to facts about alcoholism. Covers topics such as women drinkers, effects of alcohol on the body, teenage drinkers, family issues, treatment and prevention, and drinking and driving. Includes some statistics about alcohol use in Nebraska.

98. Silverstein, Alvin, and Virginia B. Silverstein. ALCOHOLISM. Philadelphia: J.B. Lippincott, 1975. 128 pp.

Presents a general discussion of alcohol covering such topics as the effects of alcohol on the body, drinking patterns, teenage drinking, drinking and driving, and the disease and treatment of alcoholism. Directed toward teenage audiences.

99. Smithers, Christopher D., Foundation. WHO ARE ALCOHOLICS? Mill Neck, N.Y.: Christopher D. Smithers Foundation, n.d. 19 pp.

Booklet uses case histories of a variety of persons (housewife, laborer, executive, homeless man, doctor, and clergyman) to illustrate that alcoholism is a disease that can afflict anyone regardless of socioeconomic background. Distinguishes between alcoholism, social drinking, and heavy drinking and lists symptoms of the early, middle, and late stages of alcoholism.

100. Solberg, Richard J. THE DRY DRUNK SYNDROME. rev. ed. Center City, Minn.: Hazelden, 1983. 12 pp.

Defines the "dry drunk syndrome" as a state of mind and pattern of behavior in the sober alcoholic which closely resembles active alcoholic behavior. Describes some of the underlying causes, symptoms, and consequences of a dry drunk and suggests resources for help for the alcoholic and his or her family.

101. Weisman, Maxwell N., and Lucy B. Robe. RELAPSE/SLIPS: ABSTINENT ALCOHOLICS WHO RETURN TO DRINKING. Minneapolis: Johnson Institute, 1983. 55 pp.

Looks at the reasons why a sober alcoholic may return to drinking. Explores the psychological problems of recovery, including denial and the "dry-drunk" syndrome. Also identifies common pitfalls or symptoms of potential return to drinking. Participation in Alcoholics Anonymous is stressed as an effective way to overcome or avoid relapse.

102. WHAT EVERYONE SHOULD KNOW ABOUT ALCOHOLISM. South Deerfield, Mass.: Channing L. Bete Co., 1981. 15 pp.

Presents a brief description of the effects of alcoholism, including the stages of alcohol addiction, long-term physiological damage, and warning signs of an alcohol problem. Suggests resources for further help and rehabilitation.

103. Wholey, Dennis, and Others. THE COURAGE TO CHANGE: HOPE AND HELP FOR ALCOHOLICS AND THEIR FAMILIES. Boston: Houghton Mifflin Co., 1984. 309 pp.

Contains descriptions by well-known personalities (such as Sid Caesar, Wilbur Mills, Gale Storm) about their alcohol problems. Also includes conversations of spouses and celebrity children of alcoholics as well as brief essays from several Alcoholics Anonymous members describing their recovery.

See also: 7, 10, 14, 17, 21, 26, 28, 29, 31, 56, 60, 66, 67, 70, 105, 107, 124, 134, 142, 260, 361, 368, 401, 403.

6. TREATMENT OF ALCOHOLISM

There are a variety of approaches to the treatment of alcoholism. This chapter contains works that describe treatment methods or programs (including many Alcoholics Anonymous publications). There are also directories of treatment facilities and materials dealing with aftercare and the recovery process. Materials for alcoholics and for therapists are included.

104. ABOUT ALCOHOLISM SERVICES. South Deerfield, Mass.: Channing L. Bete Co., 1979. 15 pp.

Offers descriptions of various types of services and facilities available for treating alcoholics. Includes such services as detoxification, health evaluation, counseling, and vocational guidance. Covers facilities such as general hospitals, outpatient clinics, mental health centers, halfway houses, and residential rehabilitation centers.

105. Alcoholics Anonymous. ALCOHOLICS ANONYMOUS: THE STORY OF HOW MANY THOUSANDS OF MEN AND WOMEN HAVE RECOVERED FROM ALCOHOLISM. 3d ed. New York: Alcoholics Anonymous World Services, 1976. 575 pp.

Nicknamed the "Big Book." Contains a history of Alcoholics Anonymous, a detailed description of the program and its components (the Twelve Steps and Twelve Traditions), and many personal accounts of alcoholism and recovery by A.A. members.

106. Alcoholics Anonymous. CAME TO BELIEVE...THE SPIRITUAL ADVENTURE OF A.A. AS EXPERIENCED BY INDIVIDUAL MEMBERS. New York: Alcoholics Anonymous World Services, 1973. 120 pp.

Describes the spiritual feelings and experiences of a number of Alcoholics Anonymous members in an effort to illustrate the importance of belief in a "higher power" to the Alcoholics Anonymous program. Focuses on crises when the alcoholic was rescued from alcoholism or relapse by faith in a higher power.

107. Alcoholics Anonymous. DO YOU THINK YOU'RE DIFFERENT? New York: Alcoholics Anonymous World Services, 1976. 30 pp.

Uses short personal accounts of a number of different members of Alcoholics Anonymous to illustrate how the A.A. program works regardless of ethnic differences, socioeconomic background, befiefs, or life style. Examples include a Black woman, a homosexual, a teenager, a clergyman, and an actress.

108. Alcoholics Anonymous. 44 QUESTIONS. New York: Alcoholics Anonymous World Services, 1952. 38 pp.

Employs a question-and-answer format to provide general information about Alcoholics Anonymous--its history, structure, membership, philosophy, and recovery program.

109. Alcoholics Anonymous. IF YOU ARE A PROFESSIONAL, A.A. WANTS TO WORK WITH YOU. New York: Alcoholics Anonymous World Services, 1972. 6 pp.

Briefly points out the benefits of cooperation between Alcoholics Anonymous and members of the professions (i.e., social workers, physicians, clergy, counselors) that deal with alcoholics. Outlines the services that A.A. and the professional community can provide for the alcoholic and answers some basic questions about the A.A. program and its effectiveness.

110. Alcoholics Anonymous. LIVING SOBER. New York: Alcoholics Anonymous World Services, 1975. 87 pp.

Offers practical advice to help recovering alcoholics maintain sobriety. Emphasizes the concepts of the Alcoholics Anonymous program and the importance of replacing old drinking-related habits. Especially helpful for newly abstinent alcoholics.

111. Alcoholics Anonymous. THIS IS A.A. New York: Alcoholics Anonymous World Services, 1953. 21 pp.

Briefly outlines the philosophy and goals of Alcoholics Anonymous. Describes the kinds of people who join A.A. and some of their basic techniques for achieving and maintaining sobriety.

112. Alcoholics Anonymous. TWELVE STEPS AND TWELVE TRADITIONS. New York: Alcoholics Anonymous World Services, 1953. 192 pp.

Explains in detail the various components of the Alcoholics Anonymous recovery program and describes the structure and functioning of the fellowship.

113. Alcoholics Anonymous. WHAT HAPPENED TO JOE AND HIS DRINKING PROBLEM.... New York: Alcoholics Anonymous World Services, 1971. 26 pp.

Uses comic-book format to tell the story of a construction worker who becomes alcoholic and recovers with the help of Alcoholics Anonymous. Illustrates the destructive effects of alcoholism on family life and job performance and provides basic information about the Alcoholics Anonymous program.

114. Alcoholics Anonymous. YOUNG PEOPLE AND A.A. New York: Alcoholics Anonymous World Services, 1969. 38 pp.

Describes how the Alcoholics Amonymous program can help young alcoholics. Offers brief accounts of the experiences of ten young alcoholics from varied social backgrounds who attained sobriety through A.A.

115. Anderson, Daniel J. PERSPECTIVES ON TREATMENT. Center City, Minn.: Hazelden, 1981. 57 pp.

Title describes the development in Minnesota of the comprehensive alcoholism treatment model. Discusses the underlying concept of alcoholism as a primary, progressive illness and emphasizes the need for a treatment program offering a wide range of services from detoxification to aftercare. Includes descriptions of four basic treatment models--detoxification programs, traditional psychiatric programs, behavior modification therapy, and the comprehensive alcoholism treatment model--and discusses some of the advantages of providing a continuum of care through a comprehensive inpatient program.

116. Bean, Margaret. OFFBEAT AND NONTRADITIONAL TREATMENT METHODS IN ALCOHOLISM. Minneapolis: Johnson Institute, 1983. 32 pp.

Describes a number of nontraditional therapies that have sometimes been applied to alcoholism and discusses their effectiveness in the prevention and recovery processes. Includes total healing systems (such as Gestalt, encounter, psychodrama and others), body manipulation techniques, meditation, and religion.

117. Brandsma, Jeffrey. OUTPATIENT TREATMENT OF ALCOHOLISM. Baltimore: University Park Press, 1980. 213 pp.

Describes and compares several of the different types of outpatient (non-institutionalized) therapy for alcoholism: insight therapy, rational behavior therapy, and Alcoholics Anonymous. All of the approaches involve some type of behavior change, group therapy, and social reinforcement for abstinence.

118. Cook, David, Christine Fewell, and John Riolo, eds. SOCIAL WORK TREATMENT OF ALCOHOL PROBLEMS. NIAAA-RUCAS Alcoholism Treatment Series, no. 5. New Brunswick, N.J.: Rutgers Center of Alcohol Studies, 1983. 153 pp.

Provides information and guidelines to assist social workers in dealing with alcoholic clients and their families. Includes chapters on screening and identification of alcoholics, matching client needs to treatment resources, different treatment approaches, and alcohol problems among several specific populations (women, adolescents, the mentally ill).

119. Estes, Nada J., Kathleen Smith-Dijulio, and M. Edith Heinemann. NURSING DIAGNOSIS OF THE ALCOHOLIC PERSON. St. Louis: C.V. Mosby Co., 1980. 251 pp.

Describes the disease of alcoholism and offers guidelines for nurses to make a medical diagnosis of the problem. Includes suggestions for conducting an interview with a suspected alcoholic and also provides diagrams and illustrations to aid in physical examination. A variety of treatment approaches are described.

120. Hazelden Foundation. COMMON SENSE FOR ALCOHOLICS. Center City, Minn.: Hazelden, 1985. 2 pp.

Presents a checklist of feelings and behaviors that alcoholics should follow during treatment and recovery. Focuses on self-examination, acceptance of the disease of alcoholism, and learning to handle everyday stresses without alcohol.

121. Hazelden Foundation. FINDING YOUR WAY: GUIDELINES FOR RECOVERY. Center City, Minn.: Hazelden, 1980. 34 pp.

Presents advice to help newly sober alcoholics during the early stages of recovery. Suggestions are based on principles of the Alcoholics Anonymous program.

122. Hazelden Foundation. WHAT IS DETOX? WHAT IS WITHDRAWAL? Center City, Minn.: Hazelden, 1985. 2 pp.

Title briefly discusses the general physical and psychological symptoms that can occur during withdrawal from alcohol, sedatives, stimulants, or opiates. Discusses how these symptoms can be safely handled under medical supervision.

123. Hoolihan, Patricia. STRESS AND RECOVERY. Center City, Minn.: Hazelden, 1984. 19 pp.

Identifies several types of stressful situations (holidays, family celebrations, hectic lifestyles) that are often encountered during recovery from alcoholism. Offers practical suggestions for handling stress through diet, exercise, relaxation, and social supports.

124. Johnson, Vernon E. I'LL QUIT TOMORROW. rev. ed. San Francisco: Harper and Row, 1980. 182 pp.

Title describes the main components of the Johnson Institute's training program for treatment of alcoholism. Contains information on blackouts, relapses, intervention, and the effects of alcoholism on family and friends. Includes a number of sample program materials such as a patient's handbook and self-evalution form, a counselor's initial interview form, a hospital personnel training handbook, and a clergyman's handbook. This should be a helpful guidebook for any professionals or paraprofessionals involved in the treatment of alcoholics.

125. Johnson Institute. ALCOHOLISM: A TREATABLE DISEASE. Minneapolis: Johnson Institute, 1972. 24 pp.

Describes alcoholism as a progressive disease which is encouraged by the alcoholic's self-delusional system. The process of intervention by family members or friends is briefly outlined.

126. Kaufman, Edward, and Pauline N. Kaufmann, eds. FAMILY THERAPY OF DRUG AND ALCOHOL ABUSE. New York: Gardner Press, 1979. 276 pp.

Discusses the benefits of treating drug and alcohol abusers through family therapy and describes several techniques such as marital group therapy and conjoint hospitalization of alcoholic and spouse. The treatment approach focuses on drug and alcohol abuse as learned behaviors and seeks to alter behavior patterns and social interactions.

127. Kurtz, Ernest. SHAME AND GUILT: CHARACTERISTICS OF THE DEPENDENCY CYCLE (AN HISTORICAL PERSPECTIVE FOR PROFESSIONALS). Professional Education Series, no. 7. Center City, Minn.: Hazelden, 1981. 57 pp.

Distinguishes between feelings of shame and guilt in alcoholics and discusses how the Alcoholics Anonymous program can be used effectively as therapy for both. Stresses the need for acceptance of human frailties and individual limitations as an important part of the alcoholic's recovery program. Booklet written for psychotherapists and other professionals involved in the rehabilitation of alcoholics.

128. M., Mary. CHOICES. Center City, Minn.: Hazelden, 1984. 17 pp.

Discusses some of the choices recovering alcoholics or drug abusers must face in order to restore harmony to their lives. Focuses on the need for self-examination and honesty in order to set realistic recovery goals rather than a pattern for failure.

129. Maxwell, Milton A. THE ALCOHOLICS ANONYMOUS EXPERIENCE: A CLOSE-UP VIEW FOR PROFESSIONALS. New York: McGraw-Hill Book Co., 1984. 174 pp.

Discusses the recovery process as experienced by members of Alcoholics Anonymous. Emphasizes the need to accept an identity as an alcoholic and stresses the importance of personal development, spiritual growth, and group involvement through the Alcoholics Anonymous program. Also includes some background on the roots of Alcoholics Anonymous and the motivations of its founders.

130. Nakken, Jane. ENABLING CHANGE: WHEN YOUR CHILD RETURNS HOME FROM TREATMENT. Center City, Minn.: Hazelden, 1985. 20 pp.

Presents guidelines for parents to help promote the successful recovery of their alcoholic or drug-addicted children. Discusses some of the difficulties that may occur in the early stages of recovery and describes several "recovery tools" (honesty, confrontation, dealing with feelings, etc.) that can help the entire family to reestablish healthy relationships.

131. Nakken, Jane. STRAIGHT BACK HOME: TO THE YOUNG PERSON LEAVING TREATMENT. Center City, Minn.: Hazelden, 1984. 15 pp.

Discusses some of the problems a young person may have to face when returning home after treatment for alcoholism or drug addiction. Describes several tools for sobriety that can help the young person with the transition back into family life. Emphasizes the importance of an aftercare plan and offers suggestions for returning to school and rebuilding social relationships.

132. National Institute on Alcohol Abuse and Alcoholism. ATTRITION FACTORS IN ALCOHOLISM TREATMENT (AFTER INITIAL CONTACT). Prepared by Ruth Bournazian. Washington, D.C.: U.S. Government Printing Office, 1983. 38 pp.

Identifies various factors (client age, sex, and race, treatment personnel characteristics, etc.) which are closely associated with an alcoholic's continuation of treatment. Offers guidelines for therapeutic techniques and outreach to motivate alcoholics toward a successful completion of treatment. Written for alcoholism counselors and other treatment staff.

133. National Institute on Alcohol Abuse and Alcoholism. TAILORING ALCOHOLISM THERAPY TO CLIENT NEEDS. Prepared by Susan D. Solomon. Washington, D.C.: U.S. Government Printing Office, 1981. 34 pp.

Designed to aid alcoholism treatment personnel in providing the best treatment approaches for their clients. Surveys existing research on measures of treatment outcome as well as client characteristics and treatment factors which can affect treatment success.

134. National Institute on Alcohol Abuse and Alcoholism. TREATING ALCOHOLISM: THE ILLNESS, THE SYMPTOMS, THE TREATMENT. Washington, D.C.: U.S. Government Printing Office, 1974. 12 pp.

Brief source offers a clear, concise explanation of alcoholism--what it is, how to recognize it, and how it affects the body and behavior. Briefly describes a variety of treatment approaches such as group therapy, family therapy, behavior and aversion therapy, and Acoholics Anonymous. Different treatment settings (hospitals, halfway houses, outpatient facilities) are also discussed, and a list of information and referral sources is included.

135. National Institute on Drug Abuse and the National Institute on Alcohol Abuse and Alcoholism. NATIONAL DIRECTORY OF DRUG ABUSE AND ALCOHOLISM TREATMENT AND PREVENTION PROGRAMS. Washington, D.C.: U.S. Government Printing Office, 1983. 301 pp.

Lists approximately 7,500 public and privately funded agencies in the U.S. and its territories that provide alcohol or drug abuse services. Entries are arranged alphabetically by city and then by title of agency within each state. Addresses and phone numbers are included, but there are no program descriptions or indication of groups served. There is a list of state alcohol and drug authorities as well as a separate directory of Veterans Administration hospitals that have alcohol or drug treatment programs.

136. Nelson, Dennis D., and Jane T. Noland. YOUNG WINNERS' WAY: A TWELVE STEP GUIDE FOR TEENAGERS. Minneapolis: CompCare Publications, 1983. 53 pp.

Short title designed for teenagers who are suffering from alcoholism. Explains each of the Twelve Steps of the Alcoholics Anonymous program in terms of adolescent feelings and experiences.

137. Rix, Keith J.B., and Elizabeth L. Rix. ALCOHOL PROBLEMS: A GUIDE FOR NURSES AND OTHER PROFESSIONALS. Bristol, England: Wright PSG, 1983. 186 pp.

Provides concise information to help nurses identify alcoholism and other alcohol-related problems among patients. Discusses some of the possible causes as well as prevalence of alcohol problems and details the symptoms of alcohol intoxication and alcohol withdrawal. Also describes a variety of medical problems that may be caused or aggravated by alcoholism, such as liver disease, gastrointestinal difficulties, and alcohol-drug interactions. There are several chapters dealing with services and techniques for intervening in alcohol problems as well as a chapter on the role of nurses (hospital and community health) in the prevention of alcoholism and alcohol abuse.

138. Shouse, Dennis W., Gregory A. Blevins, and C. Dennis Simpson. HANDBOOK FOR VOLUNTEERS IN SUBSTANCE ABUSE AGENCIES. Holmes Beach, Fla.: Learning Publications,

1983. 32 pp.

Describes a number of the roles, responsibilities, feelings, and attitudes of volunteers in alcohol and drug abuse programs. Includes an interest survey to help determine those parts of the program best suited to the volunteer's interests and also provides sample agreements between volunteers and agencies.

139. Sipe, James W. YOUTH AND A.A. Center City, Minn.: Hazelden, 1984. 17 pp.

Discusses how participation in Alcoholics Anonymous can help recovering young alcoholics deal with the pressures and problems of home, school, and social life. Explains how the A.A. program can provide support in dealing with difficult situations and in setting realistic goals and can also serve as the basis for building new social relationships.

140. Stamas, Dene. THE TRAP MAP: HOW TO TRAP THE ALCOHOLIC TO RECOVERY. Lombard, Ill.: Eureka Alcoholism Publishers, 1981. 66 pp.

Presents guidelines to help counselors motivate alcoholic clients toward recovery. Discusses methods by which therapists can avoid manipulation by clients and suggests techniques for "trapping" clients into acceptance of their alcohol problems. Explains why, when, and how to use confrontation with alcoholic clients and describes the process of "magnifying the pain" as a basic tool for alcohol counseling.

141. Staub, George E., and Leona M. Kent, eds. THE PARA-PROFESSIONAL IN THE TREATMENT OF ALCOHOLISM: A NEW PROFESSION. Springfield, Ill.: Charles C. Thomas, [1973]. 170 pp.

Title examines the role and importance of the para-professional working in an alcoholism treatment program. Focuses on attitudes toward the alcoholic as the key element in the success of a treatment program and stresses the importance of personnel training specifically geared to alcohol problems. Includes a helpful chapter on the use of non-alcoholic versus recovered personnel in a treatment program.

142. Strachan, J. George. ALCOHOLISM: TREATABLE ILLNESS. rev. ed. Center City, Minn.: Hazelden, 1982. 310 pp.

Focuses on understanding and acceptance of alcoholism as a disease which can be treated successfully. Contains information on beverage alcohol and how it affects the body and behavior. Describes different categories of drinkers (infrequent, heavy users, alcoholics) and includes a special section on youth and alcohol use. The progressive stages of alcoholism are identified, followed by an explanation of the stages of recovery. There are also chapters on counseling alcoholics, treatment of family members, the role of significant others (friends, employers, other professionals) in the identification and recovery of alcoholics, and Alcoholics Anonymous. An appendix briefly describes the warning signs of a developing dirnking problem.

143. THIRD ANNUAL NATIONAL DIRECTORY OF ALCOHOLISM AND DRUG ADDICTION TREATMENT PROGRAMS, 1984. Seattle, Wash.: Alcoholism/The National Magazine, 1984. 79 pp.

Designed to provide current information on alcoholism treatment programs and sources of alcohol information. Includes an alphabetical listing by name of treatment facility as well as a geographical listing by state and city. Contains addresses and coded information on capacity, types of services offered, length of stay, clientele, and insurance coverage. There is also a list of phone numbers for Alcoholics Anonymous central offices and intergroups, a directory of state agencies with primary responsibility for alcohol information and services, and a brief list of other national organizations and self-help groups concerned with alcohol problems.

144. THE TWELVE STEPS FOR EVERYONE...WHO REALLY WANTS THEM. Minneapolis: CompCare Publications, 1977. 128 pp.

Describes the Twelve Step program that originated with Alcoholics Anonymous and has since been adopted by a variety of self-help groups. Explains each step individually and in relation to the total program. Focuses on the Twelve Steps as a program for spiritual growth as well as recovery.

145. Weinberg, Jon R. SEX AND RECOVERY: STRAIGHT TALK FOR THE CHEMICALLY DEPENDENT AND THOSE THEY LOVE. Minneapolis: Recovery Press, 1977. 38 pp.

Identifies some of the most common sexual problems (such as guilt feelings, loss of interest or sexual ability, assertiveness, masturbation, and sexual abstinence) experienced by persons recovering from alcoholism. Suggests methods for accepting or changing sexual feelings and behaviors. Includes a list of suggested readings.

146. Woititz, Janet G. GOING HOME: A RE-ENTRY GUIDE FOR THE NEWLY SOBER. Minneapolis: CompCare Publications, 1981. 39 pp.

Offers practical suggestions to help newly recovered alcoholics readjust to family and social life after leaving a treatment setting. Covers such topics as sexual relations, handling friends and social occasions, returning to work, and slips (relapses). Emphasizes the importance of support groups such as Alcoholics Anonymous.

See also: 21, 44, 45, 56, 66, 77, 89, 91, 92, 93, 94, 95, 96, 159, 174, 180, 216, 231, 246, 267, 269, 296, 401

7. ALCOHOL PROBLEMS IN THE FAMILY

Recently much attention has been given to the problems created in the family when one or more members are alcoholic. Materials dealing with the effects of alcoholism on the family system as a whole and on individual family members are covered in this chapter. There are items that discuss the kinds of problems found in alcoholic families, items that suggest ways of coping with alcohol problems in the family, and items that focus on family therapy and recovery. Those materials that focus primarily on children of alcoholics are found in chapter eight, **Children of Alcoholics.**

147. Al-Anon Family Groups. AL-ANON FACT FILE. New York: Al-Anon Family Group Headquarters, 1972. 13 pp.

Provides a brief description of the Al-Anon (and Alateen) fellowship designed to help relatives and friends of alcoholics. Includes historical background, structure, and policies as well as a listing of the Twelve Steps and Twelve Traditions of the Al-Anon program.

148. Al-Anon Family Groups. AL-ANON: FAMILY TREATMENT TOOL IN ALCOHOLISM. rev. ed. New York: Al-Anon Family Group Headquarters, 1971. 2 pp.

Leaflet briefly outlines the structure and purposes of Al-Anon and discusses its usefulness in helping families of alcoholics. Includes statements from treatment professionals about Al-Anon's effectiveness in family therapy.

149. Al-Anon Family Groups. ALCOHOLISM: THE FAMILY DISEASE. New York: Al-Anon Family Group Headquarters, 1972. 48 pp.

Uses personal vignettes to illustrate how the Al-Anon

program can help persons cope with the alcoholism of a family member. Provides answers to commonly asked questions such as "What is alcoholism?" and "How can the family help an alcoholic?" Includes brief descriptions of the Al-Anon slogans and the Twelve Steps of the Al-Anon program.

150. Al-Anon Family Groups. THE DILEMMA OF THE ALCOHOLIC MARRIAGE. New York: Al-Anon Family Group Headquarters, 1967. 65 pp.

Examines the problems that often occur in a marriage when one of the partners is alcoholic. Focuses on problems related to sex and interpersonal communication and explains how the Al-Anon program can help the non-alcoholic partner cope with the marital situation. Also includes information about finding a local Al-Anon group.

151. Al-Anon Family Groups. A GUIDE FOR THE FAMILY OF THE ALCOHOLIC. New York: Al-Anon Family Group Headquarters, n.d. 15 pp.

Discusses the importance for the family of an alcoholic to learn as much as possible about the disease of alcoholism and about love and detachment. Includes checklists of do's and don't's for dealing with alcoholic family members.

152. Al-Anon Family Groups. LIVING WITH AN ALCOHOLIC WITH THE HELP OF AL-ANON. New York: Al-Anon Family Group Headquarters, 1960. 139 pp.

Provides in-depth information about the Al-Anon program designed to help family members cope with an alcoholic in the family. Discusses the Twelve Steps and Twelve Traditions in the Al-Anon recovery program, which can help guide family members toward an understanding of alcoholism as well as personal growth and spiritual development. Includes a chapter on Alateen--a fellowship for teenage children of alcoholics--and also contains several personal stories of Al-Anon members, including some whose spouses continued to drink. Information is also provided on the organization and procedures of Al-Anon groups.

153. Al-Anon Family Groups. "MY WIFE DRINKS TOO MUCH." New York: Al-Anon Family Group Headquarters, 1970. 11 pp.

Describes how the Al-Anon program can help husbands cope with alcoholic wives. Emphasizes acceptance of alcoholism as a disease and identifies common pitfalls to avoid when dealing with an alcoholic (e.g., covering up or making excuses for her behavior).

154. ALCOHOLIC IN THE FAMILY?....A GUIDE FOR DEALING WITH DRINKING PROBLEMS. South Deerfield, Mass.: Channing L. Bete Co., 1984. 15 pp.

Short title provides information about the effects of an individual's drinking problem on his or her family. Includes a checklist of warning signs of alcoholism as well as some common factors that may contribute to a drinking problem. Offers practical guidelines to help the family accept and cope with alcohol-related problems.

155. Boswell, Bernie, and Suzi Beeby. WHAT EVERY FAMILY SHOULD KNOW ABOUT ALCOHOLISM...OUR COMMON PROBLEM. Salt Lake City: Cottage Program International, 1982. 16 pp.

Examines the negative impact of alcoholism on family relationships and identifies four progressive stages through which families of alcoholics typically pass: denial, home treatment, chaos, control.

156. Drews, Toby R. GETTING THEM SOBER, VOLUME 1. South Plainfield, N.J.: Bridge Publishing, 1980. 204 pp.

Offers practical advice to help those (primarily spouses) who live with an active alcoholic. Covers such topics as spouse abuse, blackouts, detachment, sex, and getting help for family members. Also useful for counselors.

157. Drews, Toby R. GETTING THEM SOBER, VOLUME 1 ACTION GUIDE. South Plainfield, N.J.: Bridge Publishing, 1983. 90 pp.

Designed as companion to GETTING THEM SOBER, VOLUME 1

(no. 156). Contains suggested writing topics and other activities to correspond with chapters in the original volume. Focuses on the needs and feelings of family members (primarily spouses) of alcoholics.

158. Drews, Toby R. GETTING THEM SOBER, VOLUME 2. South Plainfield, N.J.: Bridge Publishing, 1983. 197 pp.

Offers more insights for those who live with an alcoholic to follow up the information provided in GETTING THEM SOBER, VOLUME 1 (see no. 156). Focuses on clarifying feelings and understanding alcoholic patterns. Each chapter includes suggested activities which can be used as a therapeutic or educational tool for groups or individuals.

159. Elkin, Michael. FAMILIES UNDER THE INFLUENCE: CHANGING ALCOHOLIC PATTERNS. New York: W.W. Norton and Co., 1984. 224 pp.

Describes the effects of alcoholism on the family, focusing on the roles developed by the alcoholic and nonalcoholic members. Presents a case study of a family with two substance-abusing members and discusses successful and unsuccessful techniques used by the therapist. Designed for counselors, educators, and other social service personnel who work with alcoholics and their families.

160. Forrest, Gary G. HOW TO COPE WITH A TEENAGE DRINKER: NEW ALTERNATIVES AND HOPE FOR PARENTS AND FAMILIES. New York: Atheneum, 1983. 174 pp.

Offers practical advice to parents for dealing with a teenage problem drinker. Discusses why teenagers drink and describes the behaviors and personality characteristics that are symptomatic of teenage alcohol abuse. Identifies family behaviors that may promote alcohol abuse as well as those behaviors that may inhibit abuse. Describes various treatment approaches for teenage alcoholics and also emphasizes the need for the entire family to become involved in the recovery process.

161. Forrest, Gary G. HOW TO LIVE WITH A PROBLEM DRINKER AND SURVIVE. New York: Atheneum, 1980. 117 pp.

Written to help family members or others who are close to an alcoholic. Outlines the common traits of a problem drinker and also describes the characteristics and behaviors displayed by those who live with an alcoholic. Offers specific advice for helping the alcoholic to change, including confrontation and personal detachment. Also suggests steps to help the nonalcoholic reach inner peace and satisfaction. Identifies several professional and self-help groups available for alcoholics and their families.

162. Harrison, Earl. BOOZLEBANE ON ALCOHOLISM AND THE FAMILY. Center City, Minn.: Hazelden, 1984. 21 pp.

Tongue-in-cheek spoof that illustrates the effects of alcoholism on nonalcoholic family members. Describes the feelings of shame, guilt, resentment and helplessness experienced by spouse and children and demonstrates how family members interact to perpetuate the cycle of denial and disease. Includes discussion of sexuality and intimacy in the alcoholic marriage.

163. Johnson Institute. CHEMICAL DEPENDENCY AND RECOVERY ARE A FAMILY AFFAIR. Minneapolis: Johnson Institute, 1979. 38 pp.

Written for families who have a drug or alcohol dependent member. Describes the family system as a continuum ranging from dysfunctional to nurturing, with chemical dependency seen as a disfunction. Defensive roles and coping mechanisms of family members are discussed, and helpful sections on family intervention and treatment goals are included.

164. Johnson Institute. THE FAMILY ENABLERS. Minneapolis: Johnson Institute, 1982. 19 pp.

Informative booklet describes emotions and behaviors of "enablers"--persons who are close to an alcoholic and whose actions allow the alcoholic to continue drinking. Includes a brief section on help available for enablers.

165. Johnson Institute. RECOVERY OF CHEMICALLY DEPENDENT FAMILIES. Minneapolis: Johnson Institute, n.d. 9 pp.

Discusses the most common problems faced by families with a recovering alcohol or drug abuser. Focuses on changing family roles and the need to reestablish communication. Suggests help through family counseling and support groups.

166. Keller, John E. ALCOHOL, A FAMILY AFFAIR: HELP FOR FAMILIES IN WHICH THERE IS ALCOHOL MISUSE. Santa Ynez, Calif.: The Kroc Foundation, 1977. 38 pp.

Title directed toward families in which there is alcoholism. Discusses the emotional and behavioral reactions of family members and suggests alternatives such as professional help, Al-Anon, or Alateen. A separate section is included to help the alcoholic family member assess the nature and severity of the problem.

167. Kellerman, Joseph L. ALCOHOLISM: A MERRY-GO-ROUND NAMED DENIAL. New York: Al-Anon Family Group Headquarters, 1969. 17 pp.

Discusses the role of denial in perpetuating the disease of alcoholism. Identifies three significant others--the enabler, the victim, and the "provocatrix"--who contribute to the alcoholic's denial of his disease. Describes how these persons can halt the disease process and help motivate the alcoholic into treatment. Includes a section on the pitfalls of "professional enablers" (doctors, lawyers, ministers, social workers not trained in alcoholism therapy).

168. Knowlton, Judith M., and Rebecca D. Chaitin. DETACHMENT: SEVEN SIMPLE STEPS. Rockaway, N.J.: Quotidian, 1985. 45 pp.

Outlines a seven-step process to help spouses of alcoholics detach themselves from the alcoholic system (i.e., stop reacting to the alcoholic's behavior) and focus on their own needs and emotions. Recommends regular Al-Anon participation and lists the Twelve Steps of the Al-Anon program as well as a suggested reading list and a checklist of symptoms of alcoholic behavior. The booklet is pocket-sized and provides space for individual notes.

169. Knowlton, Judith M., and Rebecca D. Chaitin. ENABLING. Rockaway, N.J.: Quotidian, 1985. 49 pp.

Describes the most common forms of enabling (actions which allow an alcoholic to continue drinking) practiced by spouses of alcoholics or others closely involved with an active alcoholic. Suggests techniques to avoid these pitfalls and includes a reading list and a checklist of symptoms of alcoholic behavior. Designed as a pocket-sized companion to DETACHMENT (no. 168).

170. LaFountain, William L. SETTING LIMITS: PARENTS, KIDS AND DRUGS. Center City, Minn.: Hazelden, 1982. 26 pp.

Combines insights and advice to help parents cope with drug or alcohol abuse by their children. Deals with parental feelings of guilt, anger, and frustration and emphasizes the need to let children suffer the consequences of their drug-related behaviors.

171. Leite, Evelyn. DETACHMENT: THE ART OF LETTING GO WHILE LIVING WITH AN ALCOHOLIC. Minneapolis: Johnson Institute, 1980. 22 pp.

Brief discussion of the negative feelings--guilt, anger, depression, low self-esteem--suffered by families of alcoholics and offers a positive alternative of detachment (shifting focus from the alcoholic to oneself). Presents a step-by-step program to implement detachment and the rebuilding of self-worth and hope.

172. Miller, Merlene, and Terence T. Gorski. FAMILY RECOVERY: GROWING BEYOND ADDICTION. Independence, Mo.: Independence Press, 1982. 69 pp.

Offers practical suggestions to help family members cope with an alcoholic. Provides information about the disease of alcoholism and the family's responses to it and emphasizes the need for nonalcoholic members to identify their own needs and to build personal strengths for coping. Also discusses how to help the alcoholic through the process of intervention and describes what to expect in the early period of recovery.

173. Mumey, Jack. SITTING IN THE BAY WINDOW: A BOOK FOR PARENTS OF YOUNG ALCOHOLICS. Chicago: Contemporary Books, 1984. 198 pp.

Offers practical advice to help parents of alcoholics understand and deal effectively with their children's alcoholism. Includes information about the disease characteristics of alcoholism and some of the genetic and psychological factors that may predispose a child toward the disease. Discusses the pitfalls of parental guilt and enabling (covering up for the alcoholic's behavior) and offers suggestions for getting help for the entire family--including the alcoholic who may not want help.

174. National Institute on Alcohol Abuse and Alcoholism. SOMEONE CLOSE DRINKS TOO MUCH. Washington, D.C.: U.S. Government Printing Office, 1974. 15 pp.

Discusses the problems of individual coping or helping a family member or close friend with a drinking problem. Outlines a three-stage helping process: learning about the illness and sources of treatment, guiding the alcoholic to treatment, and providing support during and after treatment.

175. Nebraska. Division on Alcoholism and Drug Abuse. FAMILY ABUSE AND ALCOHOL. Alcohol Effects Series. Lincoln: Nebraska Alcohol and Drug Information Clearinghouse, n.d. 3 pp.

Describes the danger of physical or verbal abuse in families where there is alcoholism. Recommends treatment for the alcoholic as well as counseling for family members.

176. Nero, Jack. IF ONLY MY WIFE COULD DRINK LIKE A LADY. Minneapolis: CompCare Publications, 1982. 312 pp.

Presents a husband's view of his wife's descent into alcoholism and her ultimate recovery. Also describes the author's development of his own disease, "mirror alcoholism," based on anger, guilt, and shame. Their recovery through the Hazelden rehabilitation program, Alcoholics Anonymous, and Al-Anon is discussed. Includes answers to questions about an alcoholic spouse's drinking behavior and also provides suggestions for dealing with a newly sober alcoholic. Written especially for husbands with alcoholic wives.

177. Pickens, Roy W., and Dace S. Svikis. ALCOHOLIC FAMILY DISORDERS: MORE THAN STATISTICS. Center City, Minn.: Hazelden, 1985. 35 pp.

Concisely identifies and describes several of the various psychological or physiological disorders that often occur in alcoholic families. These disorders may be exhibited by the alcoholic or by other members of the alcoholic's family, and they include depression, alcoholism, hysteria, eating disorders, sociopathy, fetal alcohol syndrome, and hyperactive child syndrome.

178. Porterfield, Kay M. FAMILIAR STRANGERS. Center City, Minn.: Hazelden, 1984. 145 pp.

Offers practical advice to help recovering alcoholic or drug-addicted parents rebuild positive relationships with their children. Describes some of the ways children learn to cope with their parents' addiction and suggests ways for parents to encourage new family behaviors based on communication and trust. Includes a chapter on how to talk to children about alcohol and drug use.

179. Presnall, Lewis F. ALCOHOLISM--THE EXPOSED FAMILY. 2d ed. Salt Lake City: Utah Alcoholism Foundation, 1977. 108 pp.

Thoughtful discussion of the value of Alcoholics Anonymous and similar programs for all members of an alcoholic family. Applies the Twelve Steps of Alcoholics Anonymous to family problems and relationships and emphasizes the importance of love and acceptance in family life.

180. Sauer, Joan. THE NEGLECTED MAJORITY. Milwaukee: De Paul Rehabilitation Hospital, 1976. 28 pp.

Discusses the involvement of the family in one member's alcoholism and the importance of including family members in the treatment process. Describes the effects of alcoholism on the alcoholic and on other family members and recommends further counseling and Al-Anon for family members after the alcoholic has finished treatment.

181. Smithers, Christopher D., Foundation. ALCOHOLISM: A FAMILY ILLNESS. Mill Neck, N.Y.: Christopher D. Smithers Foundation, 1984 (11th printing). 46 pp.

Presents basic information about the disease of alcoholism and how it affects family members. Describes the progression of alcoholism from early through late stages and includes a checklist of symptoms. Case histories illustrate the consequences of alcoholism to the victim, the spouse and the children.

182. Smithers, Christopher D., Foundation. ALCOHOLISM INTERVENTION: HOW TO GET A LOVED ONE INTO TREATMENT. Mill Neck, N.Y.: Christopher D. Smithers Foundation, n.d. 10 pp.

Short title offers guidelines for setting up a family confrontation to motivate an alcoholic member to seek treatment. Describes the importance of showing group concern and the need for a facilitator to insure cohesion and direction for group members. Also discusses the importance of selecting the best time for confrontation.

183. Swift, Harold A., and Terence Williams. RECOVERY FOR THE WHOLE FAMILY. Center City, Minn.: Hazelden, 1975. 16 pp.

Discusses some of the problems that family members may have to face when the alcoholic in the family recovers. Focuses on the loss of familiar roles and false esteem and suggests that nonalcoholic family members seek counseling to help adjust to the new family system.

184. Wegscheider, Sharon. ANOTHER CHANCE: HOPE AND HEALTH FOR THE ALCHOLIC FAMILY. Palo Alto, Calif.: Science and Behavior Books, 1981. 256 pp.

Examines the changes that occur in a family when a member becomes alcoholic. Defines the roles taken on by individual family members in response to the needs and actions of the alcoholic and contrasts the functioning of an alcoholic family system to that of a healthy family. Presents guidelines to help counselors intervene to restore the alcoholic family to health. This book is intended primarily for alcohol professionals but may also be helpful for suffering family members who need to understand more about the disease of alcoholism, its effects on families, and how to get help for the entire family.

185. Wegscheider, Sharon. THE FAMILY TRAP...NO ONE ESCAPES FROM A CHEMICALLY DEPENDENT FAMILY. 2d ed. Crystal, Minn.: Nurturing Networks, 1979. 17 pp.

Provides an excellent description of the various survival roles--enabler, hero, scapegoat, lost child, and mascot--adopted by members of a chemically dependent family.

186. Wegscheider-Cruse, Sharon. CHOICE-MAKING FOR CO-DEPENDENTS, ADULT CHILDREN AND SPIRITUALITY SEEKERS. Pompano Beach, Fla.: Health Communications, 1985. 206 pp.

Defines the illness of "co-dependency" (extreme dependency on another person or object) as frequently exhibited by family members of an addicted person. Describes the most common behavioral and emotional signs of co-dependency, including low self-esteem, rigidity, extreme need for approval, and difficulty expressing feelings. Focuses on several groups that have a high incidence of co-dependency: young children of alcoholics, adult children of alcoholics, and helping professionals (doctors, counselors, community workers, etc.). The goals and benefits of family therapy that deals with addiction and co-dependency are discussed along with pitfalls to avoid during the early stages of recovery. Useful for alcohol, health, or social service professionals as well as for families of alcoholics.

187. Woititz, Janet G. MARRIAGE ON THE ROCKS. New York: Delacorte Press, 1979. 148 pp.

Provides insight and coping strategies for persons with an alcoholic spouse. Discusses the effects of alcoholism and "near alcoholism" (the disease suffered by the family members) on the nonalcoholic spouse and children. Suggestions for handling guilt, fear, denial, and other negative emotional reactions are included. The emphasis is on keeping the marriage together, but the information could also be useful for parents or children of an alcoholic.

See also: 21, 66, 89, 90, 126, 146, 218, 231, 245, 392.

8. CHILDREN OF ALCOHOLICS

Items in this chapter focus specifically on children of alcoholic parents. Included are materials for young children, adolescents, and adult children. Some are also designed for use by therapists and social service workers. For items dealing with the alcoholic family as a whole, including parents and children, see chapter seven, **Alcohol Problems in the Family.**

188. Ackerman, Robert J. CHILDREN OF ALCOHOLICS: A GUIDEBOOK FOR EDUCATORS, THERAPISTS, AND PARENTS. 2d ed. Holmes Beach, Fla.: Learning Publications, 1983. 215 pp.

Examines the effects of parental alcoholism on the family as a whole and on the children in particular. Describes the family roles and perceptions of children of alcoholics as well as their physical and emotional development. Provides guidelines to help educators identify and deal effectively with children of alcoholics. Also discusses important issues in the therapy of children of alcoholics and offers suggestions for parents to help children cope with the consequences of parental alcoholism.

189. Al-Anon Family Groups. AL-ANON IS FOR ADULT CHILDREN OF ALCOHOLICS. New York: Al-Anon Family Group Headquarters, 1983. 13 pp.

Briefly illustrates some of the most significant special problems experienced by adult children of alcoholics. Gives examples to show how each of the Twelve Steps in the Al-Anon program can be used to help these victims cope with their problems.

190. Al-Anon Family Groups. AL-ANON SHARINGS FROM ADULT CHILDREN. New York: Al-Anon Family Group Headquarters, 1984. 17 pp.

Presents brief stories from fourteen adults who have alcoholic parents. Discusses how the Al-Anon program helped them deal with their parents' alcoholism and regain control over their own lives.

191. Al-Anon Family Groups. ALATEEN--HOPE FOR CHILDREN OF ALCOHOLICS. New York: Al-Anon Family Group Headquarters, 1973. 115 pp.

Explains the philosophy and workings of the Alateen program, designed to help teenagers cope with an alcoholic in the family. Discusses the basic elements of the program--the Twelve Steps, Twelve Traditions, and Slogans--and offers personal stories of teenagers who have been in the program. Also includes general information on alcoholism as well as specific informaiton on organizing Alateen groups and planning meetings.

192. Al-Anon Family Groups. FACTS ABOUT ALATEEN. New York: Al-Anon Family Group Headquarters, 1969. 2 pp.

Outlines the basic purposes and structure of the Alateen groups for teenagers who have alcoholism in their families (or among their close friends).

193. Al-Anon Family Groups. IF YOUR PARENTS DRINK TOO MUCH.... New York: Al-Anon Family Group Headquarters, 1974. 24 pp.

Depicts the problems of three teenagers who have alcoholic parents. Briefly describes the Alateen program and shows how two of the troubled teens find help for their family problems through Alateen.

194. Al-Anon Family Groups. WHATS "DRUNK," MAMA? New York: Al-Anon Family Group Headquarters, 1977. 30 pp.

Presents basic information about alcoholism for young children who have a parent with a drinking problem. Sensitively describes the reasons for the behaviors of the alcoholic and the nonalcoholic parent as well as the child's own emotional reactions. Explains briefly about the Al-Anon and Alateen programs that can help families cope with an alcoholic.

195. Al-Anon Family Groups. YOUTH AND THE ALCOHOLIC PARENT. New York: Al-Anon Family Group Headquarters, 1979. 12 pp.

Briefly describes the background and purpose of Alateen--a fellowship of children (aged 12-20) from alcoholic families. Includes answers to frequently asked questions about parental alcoholic behavior and offers suggestions for coping with family problems caused by alcohol abuse.

196. Balcerzak, Ann M. HOPE FOR YOUNG PEOPLE WITH ALCOHOLIC PARENTS. Center City, Minn.: Hazelden, 1981. 13 pp.

Written for elementary and junior high school-aged children who have an alcoholic parent. Describes alcoholism as a disease and explains why alcoholics continue to drink and how alcohol affects their behavior. Offers practical suggestions for coping with such alcohol-related problems as violence, broken promises, and embarrassing behavior by a parent. Also suggests further sources for help such as other family members, teachers and guidance counselors, clergy, and the Alateen program for teenage children of alcoholics.

197. Black, Claudia. IT WILL NEVER HAPPEN TO ME! Denver: M.A.C., 1982. 183 pp.

Focuses attention on the effects of alcoholism on the families (particularly children) of alcoholics. Identifies family roles commonly assumed by children of alcoholics, such as "the responsible one," "the adjuster," "the placater," and the "acting out" child. The effects of these childhood roles on the adult lives of the victims are also discussed, and suggestions to help identify and understand some adult behavior patterns are provided. There is also a chapter on family violence (both physical and sexual) and how to handle it. The book is especially useful for spouses and adult children of alcoholics.

198. Black, Claudia. MY DAD LOVES ME, MY DAD HAS A DISEASE. Newport Beach, Calif.: Alcoholism Children Therapy (ACT), 1979. 76 pp.

Combines illustrations with easy-to-read explanations for young children (through elementary school) with alcoholic parents. The book describes symptoms of alcoholic behavior, such as blackouts and inconsistent behavior, and helps children to examine their feelings about their alcoholic parent. There is also a section designed to help children cope with parental recovery. All illustrations are drawn by children, and blank pages are included for young readers to add their own contributions.

199. Brooks, Cathleen. THE SECRET EVERYONE KNOWS. San Diego: Operation Cork, 1981. 40 pp.

A sensitive and insightful discussion of the effects of parental alcoholism on the thoughts, feelings, and behaviors of children. Also includes basic information about the disease aspects of alcoholism and suggests strategies and resources for coping with alcohol problems.

200. Children of Alcoholics: New Jersey Task Force. CHILDREN OF ALCOHOLICS: NOBODY KNOWS MY PAIN. Rutherford, N.J.: COA-NJTF, n.d. 2 pp.

Leaflet presents a brief, helpful description of the emotional suffering of children of alcoholics and illustrates how this may affect their adult behavior.

201. Deutsch, Charles. CHILDREN OF ALCOHOLICS: UNDERSTANDING AND HELPING. Pompano Beach, Fla.: Health Communications, 1983. 12 pp.

Examines the effects of parental alcoholism on the emotional development of children. Identifies defensive roles (hero, manager, scapegoat) which children adopt in order to cope with an alcoholic family situation. Suggestions for parents, school personnel, or other concerned adults to help recognize and deal with children of alcoholics are also provided.

202. Figueroa, Ronny. PABLITO'S SECRET (EL SECRETO DE PABLITO). Pompano Beach, Fla.: Health Communications, 1984. 30 pp.

Tells the story of a child who discloses to a friend the secret of his father's drinking problem and learns about the disease of alcoholism. Written in Spanish and English for elementary school-aged children.

203. Hamilton, Dorothy. MARI'S MOUNTAIN. Scottdale, Pa.: Herald Press, 1978. 130 pp.

Recounts the various adventures of a teenage girl who leaves home to escape the physical abuse of her alcoholic father. Describes her difficulties in finding work and a place to live and deals sensitively with her reunion with her mother and the beginning of their new life together. Suitable for upper-elementary or junior high school ages (grades 5-8).

204. Hornik-Beer, Edith L . A TEENAGER'S GUIDE TO LIVING WITH AN ALCOHOLIC PARENT. Center City, Minn.: Hazelden, 1984. 83 pp.

Answers questions from teenage children of alcoholics about their parents' alcoholic behaviors and their own related feelings and experiences. Covers such topics as bringing friends home, sharing family responsibilities, getting help to cope with parental alcoholism, and what to expect from a newly-sober parent.

205. Kenny, Kevin, and Helen Krull. SOMETIMES MY MOM DRINKS TOO MUCH. Milwaukee: Raintree Childrens Books, 1980. 31 pp.

Describes the difficulties a young girl experiences as a result of her mother's drinking problem. Explains that alcoholism is a disease that is no one's fault and suggests persons (other family members, teachers) that may be able to help a child understand and cope. Written for younger elementary school-aged children. Illustrated.

206. National Institute on Alcohol Abuse and Alcoholism. A GROWING CONCERN: HOW TO PROVIDE SERVICES FOR CHILDREN

FROM ALCOHOLIC FAMILIES. Prepared by Barbara J. Waite and Meredith J. Ludwig. Washington, D.C.: U.S. Government Printing Office, 1983. 52 pp.

Identifies problems and needs experienced by children of alcoholics and explores a variety of approaches and caregivers to serve this population. Also examines special needs and services for ethnic and cultural groups (Blacks, Hispanics, Native Americans). Includes a reading list and descriptions of several programs (in schools, communities, and treatment settings) dealing with children of alcoholics.

207. Oppenheimer, Joan L. FRANCESCA, BABY. New York: Scholastic Book Services, 1976. 156 pp.

Absorbing and moving fictional account of a teenage girl's difficulties in coping with her alcoholic mother. Focuses on problems with family and social relationships and incorporates helpful information about Alateen, Al-Anon, and Alcoholics Anonymous. Written for junior and senior high school students.

208. Pickens, Roy W. CHILDREN OF ALCOHOLICS. Center City, Minn.: Hazelden, 1984. 25 pp.

Identifies four disorders that may be found in children of alcoholics and describes the symptoms and possible treatment or prevention for each: fetal alcohol syndrome, hyperactive child syndrome, adult alcoholism, and adult depression.

209. Robe, Lucy B. HAUNTED INHERITANCE. Minneapolis: CompCare Publications, 1980. 160 pp.

Includes mystery, suspense, romance, and information about alcoholism within the tale of a young woman's unusual inheritance. Contains some discussion of the disease aspect of alcoholism and its effects on the family (including fetal alcohol syndrome). Interesting reading for teenagers.

210. Seixas, Judith S., and Geraldine Youcha. CHILDREN OF ALCOHOLISM: A SURVIVOR'S MANUAL. New York: Crown Publishers, 1985. 208 pp.

Written for and about adult children of alcoholics. Uses case histories to describe the experiences and feelings common to many children who grew up in alcoholic homes and discusses the effects of these experiences on adult lifestyles and relationships. Offers sensitive and practical advice for coping with these effects of alcoholism and for dealing with other family members, including children and alcoholic parents. Includes resources for further reading, information, and help.

211. Typpo, Marion H., and Jill M. Hastings. AN ELEPHANT IN THE LIVING ROOM. 2 vols. Minneapolis: CompCare Publications, 1984. 69 pp. (plus leader's guide, 124 pp.)

Designed to help elementary school-aged children from families in which there is an alcohol or drug abusing member. The set includes a children's workbook with activities to help children understand and express their feelings, improve self-esteem and family relationships, and cope with problems caused by alcoholism or drug abuse. There is also a leader's guide for use by adult professionals, including counselors, teachers, and social workers. The guide contains information on the disease of alcoholism, family roles and models, child development (physical and social), and providing help in a variety of settings--schools, treatment centers, support groups--for children of alcoholics.

212. Woititz, Janet G. ADULT CHILDREN OF ALCOHOLICS. Pompano Beach, Fla.: Health Communications, 1983. 106 pp.

Written for adults who have grown up in homes with parental alcoholism. The author identifies thirteen "generalizations" regarding the emotional and psychological functioning of these adults (for example, difficulty with intimate relationships, impulsive behavior, and constant need for approval). Suggestions for dealing with negative feelings and established behavior patterns are offered. This book would also be useful for counselors dealing with such individuals.

213. Woititz, Janet G. ADULT CHILDREN OF ALCOHOLICS: COMMON CHARACTERISTICS. Pompano Beach, Fla.: Health Communications, 1983. 12 pp.

Identifies and briefly discusses some of the most common behaviors and characteristics of adult children of alcoholics. Emphasizes the role of childhood experience in an alcoholic home in contributing to negative behaviors and self-image in adulthood.

See also: 245, 360.

9. ALCOHOL USE AMONG WOMEN

There is a growing body of literature focusing specifically on the problems and needs of women regarding alcohol use. This chapter covers the effects of alcohol on women, reasons why women develop alcohol problems, and alcohol treatment needs and approaches for women.

214. ABOUT WOMEN AND ALCOHOL. South Deefield, Mass.: Channing L. Bete Co., 1980. 15 pp.

Focuses on the special problems of alcoholism among women. Outlines some of the factors related to female alcohol abuse, including marital and family problems, low self-image, loss of loved ones, and sexual problems. Briefly describes the warning signs of a drinking problem and offers suggestions for family support and sources of help.

215. Alcohol and Drug Problems Association. SOME THOUGHTS ABOUT DRINKING FOR WOMEN IN THE WORKPLACE. Washington, D.C.: Alcohol and Drug Problems Association of North America, 1984. 13 pp.

Discusses drinking practices and effects of alcohol on women, focusing on the special aspects of alcohol use among working women. Identifies possible causes and symptoms of alcohol abuse by working women and includes suggestions for getting help.

216. Alcoholics Anonymous. IT HAPPENED TO ALICE!...HOW SHE FACED A DRINKING PROBLEM. New York: Alcoholics Anonymous World Services, 1971. 26 pp.

Uses comic book format to describe the crisis reached by an alcoholic housewife and her subsequent recovery through the Alcoholics Anonymous program. Aimed particularly toward young married women.

217. Casey, Therese. PMS AND ALCOHOLISM. Center City, Minn.: Hazelden, 1984. 18 pp.

Booklet describes the common symptoms of premenstrual syndrome (PMS) and discusses the similarity to the "dry drunk" syndrome or alcoholic behavior. Offers practical suggestions (diet and vitamin therapy, exercise, stress management) to help alleviate the negative effects of PMS.

218. Curlee-Salisbury, Joan. WHEN THE WOMAN YOU LOVE IS AN ALCOHOLIC. St. Meinrad, Ind.: Abbey Press, 1978. 96 pp.

Provides information about alcoholism for family members and close friends of women alcoholics. Describes symptoms and contributing factors to alcoholism in women and focuses on denial as the main obstacle to recovery. Identifies a variety of resources available for the alcoholic and family members.

219. Cusack, Suzanne B. WOMEN AND RELAPSE. Center City, Minn.: Hazelden, 1984. 34 pp.

Examines the emotional and physiological problems commonly associated with women's return to active alcoholism. Stresses the importance of bolstering female self-esteem and providing adequate and genuine emotional support systems immediately after relapse.

220. Eddy, Cristen C., and John L. Ford, eds. ALCOHOLISM IN WOMEN. Dubuque, Iowa: Kendall/Hunt Publishing Co., 1980. 189 pp.

Examination of the prevalence and characteristics of alcohol problems among women and suggests techniques and approaches for the prevention and treatment of these problems. Identifies many of the social and psychological factors that may lead to female alcoholism and discusses methods of prevention or early intervention for alcohol problems. A section on treatment covers diagnosis and casefinding as well as various therapeutic approaches that focus specifically on women. Suitable for college students, social service workers, or alcohol treatment personnel.

221. Gust, Dodie. CAREER WOMAN/ GOING UP FAST: ALCOHOLIC/ GOING DOWN FAST. Minneapolis: CompCare Publications, 1977. 22 pp.

Depicts the problems of female alcoholics in the workplace, using several examples: a school teacher, an information specialist, a secretary, and an office manager. Discusses some of the factors which influence female drinking and describes how employee assistance programs can help to identify and rehabilitate female alcoholics.

222. Hazelden Foundation. LEARN ABOUT WOMEN AND ALCOHOL. Hazelden Learn About Series. Center City, Minn.: Hazelden, 1984. 15 pp.

Provides useful information about the drinking habits and practices of women along with the effects of alcohol on the female body. Discusses some of the different effects of alcohol on women and men (including effects of the menstrual cycle and oral contraceptives) and also corrects some common misinformation about female alcohol use.

223. Johnson Institute. WOMEN, ALCOHOL AND DEPENDENCY: I AM RESPONSIBLE. Minneapolis, Minn.: Johnson Institute, 1981. 23 pp.

Discusses the symptoms and consequences of alcoholism including those manifestations found most often in women. Briefly describes the process of intervention as practiced by family, friends, or employers of alcoholic women. Outlines the special problems and needs of women during treatment and recovery from alcoholism, with emphasis on the enhancement of self-esteem.

224. Kimball, Bonnie-Jean. THE ALCOHOLIC WOMAN'S MAD, MAD WORLD OF DENIAL AND MIND GAMES. Center City, Minn.: Hazelden, 1978. 69 pp.

Focuses on the process of denial which worsens alcohol problems among women and impedes recovery. Examines mind games ("unhealthy mental concepts which prevent recovery") and defense mechanisms employed by women alcoholics and concerned others--family, friends, professionals (doctors, clergy, law enforcement, etc.). Describes the recovery process and offers guidelines for effective intervention by concerned persons.

225. Kimball, Bonnie-Jean. THE WOMAN ALCOHOLIC AND HER TOTAL RECOVERY PROGRAM. Center City, Minn.: Hazelden, 1976. 21 pp.

Describes the problems frequently encountered by recovering women alcoholics. Includes a detailed example of the kind of negative thinking that can destroy new sobriety.

226. Kirkpatrick, Jean. A FRESH START. Dubuque, Iowa: Kendall/Hunt, 1981. 164 pp.

Offers description of how and why Women for Sobriety, a self-help recovery group for women alcoholics, was founded. Discusses the author's own alcoholism and her formula for recovery, which formed the basis for the program.

227. Kirkpatrick, Jean. TURNABOUT: HELP FOR A NEW LIFE. Dubuque, Iowa: Kendall/Hunt, 1977. 183 pp.

Description of the author's personal struggles with alcoholism and her subsequent recovery and founding of Women for Sobriety, a self-help program for women alcoholics. Explains in detail the program's Thirteen Statements of Acceptance, which provide a model to help women alcoholics reshape their lives.

228. Lindbeck, Vera. THE WOMAN ALCOHOLIC. Public Affairs Pamphlet, No. 529. New York: Public Affairs Committee, 1975. 28 pp.

Short title describes the problems experienced by women alcoholics, using several case histories as examples. Some factors particularly associated with the development of female alcoholism are discussed, and several signs of a hidden alcohol problem are outlined. There are suggestions to help family members and friends deal with the alcoholic, and several types of resources available to help alcoholic women are briefly described.

229. McConville, Brigid. WOMEN UNDER THE INFLUENCE: ALCOHOL AND ITS IMPACT. London: Virago Press, 1983. 151 pp.

Discusses patterns and extent of alcohol use among contemporary women. Identifies some of the reasons why women drink, as well as how, when, and where they do their drinking, and relates these factors to the most frequently depicted stereotypes of women drinkers. Provides information on how alcohol affects the female body, including a chapter devoted to the risks of alcohol use during pregnancy. There is also a section on identifying alcohol problems and getting help. Although written especially for women in Great Britain, the information in this book is equally valid and useful for women in the United States.

230. McGuire, Patricia C. THE LIBERATED WOMAN. Center City, Minn.: Hazelden, 1977. 15 pp.

Examines the differences between chemically dependent women and men. Describes three general groups of women substance abusers--early problem drinkers, middle-aged alcoholics, and prescription drug addicts--and discusses personality characteristics and factors leading to addiction. Also explores typical female dependency roles and social stereotypes which contribute to low self-esteem and substance abuse. Liberation is defined as freedom from chemical dependency and negative lifestyles and is offered as a positive alternative to regain self-respect and healthy relationships with friends and family.

231. Meryman, Richard. BROKEN PROMISES, MENDED DREAMS. Boston: Little, Brown and Co., 1984. 351 pp.

Fictional account of the suffering of a housewife addicted to alcohol, her decision to seek treatment, and her ultimate recovery. Looks at the suffering of her husband and teenage children and describes the family's readjustment to a sober wife and mother. Provides a detailed account of the rehabilitation process, including family therapy sessions.

232. National Institute on Alcohol Abuse and Alcoholism. ALCOHOL ABUSE AND WOMEN: A GUIDE TO GETTING HELP. Prepared by Marian Sandmaier. Washington, D.C.: U.S.

Government Printing Office, 1976. 25 pp.

Presents a well-written overview of alcohol problems among women. Explores some of the reasons why women develop drinking problems (job pressure, loneliness, role conflict, etc.) and why they often do not seek treatment. A discussion of the treatment process, with emphasis on Alcoholics Anonymous, is included as is a list of other resources for help or information. A checklist of symptoms of a developing drinking problem is also provided.

233. National Institute on Alcohol Abuse and Alcoholism. FOR WOMEN WHO DRINK.... Washington, D.C.: U.S. Government Printing Office, 1982. 12 pp.

Describes some of the reasons and emotions associated with alcohol use by women and includes a list of questions to help diagnose a possible drinking problem. Briefly discusses the goals and types of treatment available to women.

234. Porterfield, Kay. SOBER AND SENSUAL. Center City, Minn.: Hazelden, 1985. 36 pp.

Presents a frank discussion of sexual problems (sex roles, sexual functioning) that many alcoholic women experience after attaining sobriety. Suggests ways of identifying sexual fears and communicating physical and emotional needs to sex partners.

235. Rebeta-Burditt, Joyce. THE CRACKER FACTORY. New York: Collier, 1977. 312 pp.

Depicts the (fictional) problems and recovery of a suburban housewife struggling with alcoholism. Describes her refusal to accept her disease, her treatment in psychiatric hospitals, her problems with family relationships, and her difficult road back toward self-respect and abstinence. This book is humorous, candid, and sensitive.

236. Sandmaier, Marian. HELPING WOMEN WITH ALCOHOL PROBLEMS. Philadelphia: Women's Health Communications, 1982. 40 pp.

Offers advice to help social service personnel (e.g.,

family and job counselors, nurses, clergy, doctors, social workers) identify alcohol problems among women clients. Includes background information on the scope and consequences of alcohol problems and presents guidelines for intervention and referral. Suggestions to support the recovering woman alcoholic as well as lists of resources for further information are also presented.

237. Sandmaier, Marian. THE INVISIBLE ALCOHOLICS: WOMEN AND ALCOHOL ABUSE IN AMERICA. New York: McGraw-Hill, 1980. 298 pp.

Presents a good overview of the problem of alcohol abuse among women, including attitudes toward alcohol use as well as drinking patterns. Alcohol problems among several sub-groups--housewives, employed women, minority women, teenage girls, lesbians, and women on Skid Row--are discussed, and suggestions on how and where to get treatment are provided. The emphasis is on alcoholism as a disease that has separate and unique origins for women and men.

238. Youcha, Geraldine. A DANGEROUS PLEASURE. New York: Hawthorn Books, 1978. 251 pp.

Discusses how and why women use alcoholic beverages as well as the long- and short-term effects of alcohol on the body and the brain. Identifies certain alcohol problems that are peculiar to women, such as the relationship between hormone levels and alcoholism and the risks of alcohol use during pregnancy. Describes a variety of treatment approaches that have been used for women and includes a list of treatment and information sources. Also includes guidelines for sensible drinking habits and a checklist of alcoholism symptoms.

See also: 89, 153, 176, 268, 306, 324.

10. ALCOHOL USE AMONG YOUTH

In the recently published FIFTH SPECIAL REPORT TO CONGRESS ON ALCOHOL AND HEALTH the National Institute on Alcohol Abuse and Alcoholism estimated that over three million young people have problems related to alcohol use. These problems include highway accidents, delinquency, family or school difficulties, and alcoholism. Many of the items in this chapter are written for adults--parents, teachers, therapists, youth workers--about the nature and prevalence of alcohol problems among youth and how to treat or prevent them. In addition there are a number of materials written for young people themselves about physical, behavioral, and social consequences of alcohol use. Also included are several fictional accounts of teenage alcoholics. Materials for or about college students are covered in this chapter as well.

239. Alcoholics Anonymous. TOO YOUNG? New York: Alcoholics Anonymous World Services, 1977. 18 pp.

Uses comic book format to present the stories of six alcoholic teenagers who turned to Alcoholics Anonymous for help. Includes a checklist of symptoms to help teenagers evaluate their own drinking patterns.

240. Barnes, Grace M. ALCOHOL AND YOUTH: A COMPREHENSIVE BIBLIOGRAPHY. Westport, Conn.: Greenwood Press, 1982. 452 pp.

Contains nearly 5,000 citations to books, journal articles, theses, government reports, and popular literature dealing with alcohol use among youth. Items cover a variety of aspects such as prevalence studies, college students, alcohol-related problems, and prevention and public policy issues. Entries are arranged alphabetically by author with a subject index. Both English and foreign-language documents are included.

241. Bean, Margaret. ALCOHOL AND ADOLESCENTS: IDENTIFYING AND MANAGING THE PROBLEMS. Minneapolis: Johnson Institute, 1982. 23 pp.

Presents guidelines to aid physicians in identifying and handling adolescent patients who are suffering from alcohol problems. Distinguishes between experimentation, problem drinking, and alcoholism and offers case histories as examples. Suggested resources for referral of adolescents with drinking problems are included.

242. Claypool, Jane. ALCOHOL AND YOU. New York: Franklin Watts, 1981. 84 pp.

Presents information for teenagers about alcohol use and alcohol problems. Discusses why teenagers drink alcohol, how alcohol affects the body and behavior, how alcoholism develops, and where to get help for alcohol problems. Includes a list of resources for further information and a brief reading list.

243. Cross, Wilbur. KIDS AND BOOZE: WHAT YOU MUST KNOW TO HELP THEM. New York: E.P. Dutton, 1979. 180 pp.

Presents basic information to parents and educators about adolescent alcohol use and abuse. Identifies communication "roadblocks" between parents and children and offers helpful guidelines for teaching young people to make responsible decisions about alcohol use. Several alcohol education programs for school, church, and community are briefly described.

244. Donlan, Joan. I NEVER SAW THE SUN RISE. Minneapolis: CompCare Publications, 1977. 199 pp.

Diary of a teenage girl's addiction to drugs and alcohol. Describes her experiences, perceptions, and emotional reactions during her chemical dependency and also during her treatment and recovery. Provides insight into some of the reasons for teenage addiction.

245. Greene, Shep. THE BOY WHO DRANK TOO MUCH. New York: Viking Press, 1979. 149 pp.

Tells the fictional story of a teenage hockey player's problems with alcohol and his eventual decision to seek help. Focuses on the boy's relationship with his drunken, abusive father and his social isolation as factors contributing to the development of his own drinking problem.

246. Griffin, Tom, and Roger Svendsen. THE STUDENT ASSISTANCE PROGRAM: HOW IT WORKS. Center City, Minn.: Hazelden, 1980. 60 pp.

Outlines a program designed to help students and school staff deal with problems (physiological, psychological, alcohol, drug, etc.) that are interfering with school performance. Based on the standard model of employee assistance programs used in many businesses. Includes chapters on policy development, roles and responsibilities of those involved (teachers, administrators, student assistance assessment team), and the role of the school in prevention of alcohol, drug, and other mental health problems. A number of sample materials are also provided, such as an agency referral checklist and sample policies with program outlines. This model could be easily adapted to a variety of school settings.

247. Haskins, Jim. TEEN-AGE ALCOHOLISM. New York: Hawthorn Books, 1976. 156 pp.

Examines the facts and popular fallacies about teenage alcohol use and abuse. Includes a good deal of background material on the uses of alcohol throughout history with particular focus on the evolution of American drinking practices and social attitudes. Describes the effects of alcohol on the body and on behavior and discusses the consequences of long-term alcohol abuse by teenagers. Identifies the most common reasons for teenage drinking (parental and social pressures, peer pressure, emotional problems, and the effect of feeling good) and suggests ways for parents and concerned persons to deal with alcohol problems. Suitable for teenagers and their parents.

248. Hazelden Foundation. NEVER TOO EARLY, NEVER TOO LATE: A BOOKLET FOR PARENTS AND OTHERS CONCERNED ABOUT DRUG

AND ALCOHOL USE PROBLEMS. Center City, Minn.: Hazelden, 1983. 19 pp.

Explores motives for alcohol and other drug use by young people. Includes warning signs of an alcohol or drug problem and guidelines to help parents deal with these problems.

249. Krupski, Ann M. INSIDE THE ADOLESCENT ALCOHOLIC. Center City, Minn.: Hazelden, 1982. 66 pp.

Describes the symptoms of alcohol addiction in adolescents and identifies five stages--denial, anger, bargaining, depression, and acceptance--in the parents' and the adolescent's reaction to a diagnosis of alcoholism. Offers guidelines to facilitate family recovery.

250. Macdonald, Donald I. DRUGS, DRINKING AND ADOLESCENTS. Chicago: Year Book Medical Publishers, 1984. 200 pp.

Examination of trends in drug and alcohol use by adolescents and discusses the importance of identification, treatment, and prevention of substance abuse problems among youth. Describes the stages of drug use from curiosity to dependency and also looks at the physiological effects of a variety of popular drugs, including alcohol. There are examples of parent-group actions against alcohol and drug abuse as well as guidelines to help physicians in the diagnosis and treatment of these problems. Appendixes contain suggested parent-teen guidelines for social life outside of school and an instrument to help parents identify possible drug problems in their children.

251. Maddox, George L., ed. THE DOMESTICATED DRUG: DRINKING AMONG COLLEGIANS. New Haven, Conn.: College and University Press, 1970. 470 pp.

Examines college drinking practices up to 1970, including information on the social context of student drinking as well as the effects of drinking on the body and the mind. There is a review of general population surveys associating drinking with educational level and also a section of empirical studies dealing with drinking behaviors and patterns and the relationship of drinking to personality needs. The importance of university policies regarding student drinking is stressed, and guidelines are included for educators and administrators interested in setting up an alcohol education program.

252. Marshall, Shelley. YOUNG, SOBER AND FREE. Center City, Minn.: Hazelden, 1978. 137 pp.

Presents the personal stories of addiction and recovery of several young alcohol and drug abusers. An explanation of the Twelve Steps of Alcoholics Anonymous is included. There is also a section written "to parents, by parents," which describes the problems they faced and how they learned to deal with them through the help of Al-Anon, Alcoholics Anonymous, and Narcotics Anonymous.

253. Milgram, Gail G. WHAT, WHEN, AND HOW TO TALK TO CHILDREN ABOUT ALCOHOL AND OTHER DRUGS: A GUIDE FOR PARENTS. Center City, Minn.: Hazelden, 1983. 87 pp.

Designed as a basic guidebook to help parents encourage responsible decisions by adolescents regarding alcohol and other drug use. Provides information on how and why people use alcohol and drugs, including appendixes which briefly describe the effects of various substances on the body and on behavior, as well as problems related to alcohol and drug use. There is a very helpful section with suggested techniques to facilitate communication between parents and children. A bibliography and list of resources are also included.

254. National Institute on Alcohol Abuse and Alcoholism. YOUNG PEOPLE AND ALCOHOL: DRINKING PRACTICES, DRINKING PROBLEMS, INITIATIVES IN PREVENTION AND TREATMENT. Washington, D.C.: U.S. Government Printing Office, 1975. 10 pp.

Looks at trends in alcohol use and abuse by young people and describes several prevention and education programs which deal with alcohol concerns. Also includes brief descriptions of several treatment programs geared toward young alcohol abusers. Reprinted from ALCOHOL HEALTH AND RESEARCH WORLD, summer 1975.

255. North, Robert, and Richard Orange, Jr. TEENAGE DRINKING: THE #1 DRUG THREAT TO YOUNG PEOPLE TODAY. New York: Macmillan, 1980. 144 pp.

Presents information for teenagers about alcohol use and alcohol problems. Discusses why teenagers drink, how alcohol affects the body, and the negative consequences that can result from alcohol abuse. Offers suggestions for avoiding excessive alcohol use and for helping a friend with an alcohol problem. The appendixes contain suggested activities, strategies, and resources to help adults (i.e., parents, educators, community workers) plan effective alcohol prevention programs.

256. Peele, Stanton. DON'T PANIC! A PARENT'S GUIDE TO UNDERSTANDING AND PREVENTING ALCOHOL AND DRUG ABUSE. Minneapolis: CompCare Publications, 1983. 37 pp.

Discusses the importance of parental role modeling and support in preventing alcohol and drug problems among adolescents. Stresses the need for open communication, good health practices, and values and attitudes based on a positive self-image and outlook toward life. Includes information on why kids drink and use drugs and examines some of the reasons why traditional prevention and treatment approaches have often failed.

257. Saltman, Jules. TEENAGERS AND ALCOHOL: PATTERNS AND DANGERS. Public Affairs Pamphlet, No. 612. New York: Public Affairs Committee, 1983. 29 pp.

Looks at problems which may be associated with teenage alcohol use--particularly alcoholism, aggressive behavor (violent or sexual), and drunk driving. Discusses various approaches (legal measures, school and community prevention programs) which have been used to deal with these alcohol problems. There are brief descriptions of several alcohol treatment programs especially for youth as well as descriptions of a number of prevention programs in communities and on college campuses.

258. Smart, Reginald G. THE NEW DRINKERS: TEENAGE USE AND ABUSE OF ALCOHOL. 2d ed. Toronto: Addiction Research Foundation, 1980. 180 pp.

Discusses the extent of alcohol use and alcohol problems among young people and suggests ways in which parents, schools, and governments can help prevent these problems. Includes a chapter on the effects of changing the minimum drinking-age laws in Canada and the United States. There is an extensive reference list of published research studies as well as resource lists of print and audiovisual materials for students and adults.

259. Snyder, Anne. KIDS AND DRINKING. Minneapolis: Comp-Care Publications, 1977. 47 pp.

Presents three case histories of young alcoholics who began their drinking in their pre-teen years. Includes a twenty-question self-test to help young persons determine if they are developing a drinking problem. Also contains basic information about alcoholism as a disease. There is a brief section with suggestions for parents and teachers to stimulate discussion about alcohol use by young people. Suitable for elementary and junior high audiences.

260. Snyder, Anne. MY NAME IS DAVY. I'M AN ALCOHOLIC. New York: New American Library, 1977. 134 pp.

Depicts the onset and progression of alcoholism in a 15-year-old boy and describes the crisis which leads him toward recovery in Alcoholics Anonymous. Focuses on factors such as loneliness and peer acceptance which contribute to teenage alcohol use and illustrates many of the negative consequences of youthful drinking behavior. Also deals frankly with teenage sexual behavior and its relationship to alcohol use.

261. Wagner, Robin S. SARAH T.: PORTRAIT OF A TEEN-AGE ALCOHOLIC. New York: Ballantine Books, 1975. 120 pp.

Describes the problems of a lonely teenage girl who turns to alcohol to cope with her problems. Depicts the rapid, often violent, descent into teenage alcoholism and illustrates the difficulty for victim and family of accepting and dealing with the problem.

262. WHAT EVERY TEENAGER SHOULD KNOW ABOUT ALCOHOL. South Deerfield, Mass.: Channing L. Bete Co., 1980. 15 pp.

Presents basic information for teenagers about the effects of alcohol on the body and on behavior. Outlines problems (behavioral, physical, emotional, sexual, academic, and legal) which can result from the abuse of alcohol and offers guidelines for making responsible decisions about alcohol use.

263. WHAT YOU SHOULD KNOW ABOUT ALCOHOL ON CAMPUS. South Deerfield, Mass.: Channing L. Bete Co., 1982. 15 pp.

Examines briefly the use of alcohol by college students. Describes the effects of alcohol on the body and on behavior and identifies personal and social problems that may result from alcohol abuse. Includes a checklist of warning signs for alcohol problems as well as suggestions for where to get help.

264. Yoast, Richard, Cindy Scott, Lynn Tolcott, and others. YOU ASKED FOR IT: INFORMATION ON ALCOHOL, OTHER DRUGS AND TEENAGERS. Madison: Wisconsin Clearinghouse, 1981. 24 pp.

Provides information about the effects of alcohol and other drugs (including marijuana, stimulants, cocaine, hallucinogens, and tobacco) on the body. Also explores special issues such as the effects of drugs and alcohol on sex, reproduction, driving ability, school performance, and sports. Offers suggestions for dealing with friends or parents who have some type of drug problem and includes a checklist of symptoms for self-diagnosis of substance abuse.

265. THE YOUNG DRINKERS: TEENAGERS AND ALCOHOL. Pompano Beach, Fla.: Health Communications, n.d. 12 pp.

Focuses on the problems associated with alcohol and other drug use by teenagers. Includes statistics on drinking and drug using patterns as well as problems such as drunk-driving accidents. Symptoms of an alcohol or drug problem are briefly outlined, and suggestions for preventing and dealing with such problems are offered.

See also: 66, 89, 114, 130, 131, 136, 139, 160, 170, 173, 347, 356, 362, 363, 379.

11. ALCOHOL USE AMONG SPECIAL POPULATIONS

Researchers have documented the effects of social and cultural experiences on drinking practices. This chapter cites works that deal with alcohol use and alcohol problems within special population groups: minorities (Blacks, American Indians, Hispanic Americans), the elderly, homosexuals, Skid Row residents, and certain occupational groups. Because popular publications on some of these groups, such as American Indians and Hispanics, are scarce, several research studies and reviews have been included to provide the user with adequate information in these areas. Research bibliographies on several population groups have also been published as part of the ALCOHOL BIBLIOGRAPHY SERIES (no. 1).

266. Alcoholics Anonymous. A.A. AND THE ARMED SERVICES. New York: Alcoholics Anonymous World Services, 1974. 30 pp.

Presents the brief stories of ten military personnel who overcame their drinking problems through the Alcoholics Anonymous program. Also answers several questions of concern to military members of Alcoholics Anonymous, such as whether advancement may be affected or how to find an A.A. meeting in remote areas.

267. Allen, Chaney. I'M BLACK AND I'M SOBER. Minneapolis: CompCare Publications, 1978. 279 pp.

Presents a moving account of the author's descent into alcoholism and her eventual treatment and recovery. Depicts the family, economic, and physical problems associated with alcoholism and describes the problems and triumphs of recovery through Alcoholics Anonymous.

268. Arevalo, Rodolfo, and Marianne Minor, eds. CHICANAS AND ALCOHOLISM: A SOCIO-CULTURAL PERSPECTIVE OF WOMEN. San Jose, Calif.: School of Social Work, San Jose State University, 1981. 55 pp.

Short monograph designed to provide social work students with increased knowledge about alcohol problems among minority women (with special emphasis on Hispanic women). Presents guidelines for planning and delivering more effective treatment and prevention programs to meet the special needs of these groups.

269. Bell, Peter, and Jimmy Evans. COUNSELING THE BLACK CLIENT. Professional Education Series, No. 5. Center City, Minn.: Hazelden, 1981. 43 pp.

Discusses the effects of alcoholism on the Black community and offers guidelines for more effective counseling of Black alcoholics. Identifies personal values and professional techniques in White as well as Black counselors that can inhibit treatment success and suggests ways of overcoming counselor and client obstacles to treatment.

270. Bissell, LeClair, and Paul Haberman. ALCOHOLISM IN THE PROFESSIONS. New York: Oxford University Press, 1984. 214 pp.

Presents data from a study of alcoholics in a variety of professions (health and dental care, social service, law). Explores not only the prevalence of alcohol problems within different professions but also the incidence of relapse. Includes valuable information on professional organizations and self-help groups available to aid alcohol-impaired professionals.

271. Blumberg, Leonard U., Thomas Shipley, Jr., and Stephen F. Barsky. LIQUOR AND POVERTY: SKID ROW AS A HUMAN CONDITION. Monographs of the Rutgers Center of Alcohol Studies, No. 13. New Brunswick, N.J.: Rutgers Center of Alcohol Studies, 1978. 289 pp.

Important sociological study describes Skid Row as an identifiable lifestyle characterized by homelessness, poverty, and certain drinking behaviors (such as binge drinking and bottle gangs). Presents an in-depth examination of the Skid Rows of Philadelphia, Detroit, and San Francisco and also looks at particular Skid Row populations, including Blacks and women. Contains recommendations for serving the social, economic, and residential needs of Skid Row persons as well as for preventing the development of future Skid Rows.

272. Buys, Donna, and Jules Saltman. THE UNSEEN ALCOHOLICS--THE ELDERLY. Public Affairs Pamphlet, No. 602. New York: Public Affairs Committee, 1982. 24 pp.

Describes the various symptoms and contributing factors (loneliness, declining health, etc.) of alcoholism among elderly persons. Offers guidelines for motivating the elderly alcoholic into treatment and discusses problems that may arise in the recovery process.

273. Carle, Cecil E. LETTERS TO ELDERLY ALCOHOLICS: SHARING THE SOLUTION AND THE PROBLEM. Center City, Minn.: Hazelden, 1980. 89 pp.

Uses personal letters as a format to break through the denial system of elderly persons with alcohol problems. Discusses some of the signs and contributing factors of alcoholism, focusing on the special needs and problems of the elderly. Offers suggestions for getting help, including advice for the friends of elderly alcoholics.

274. Day-Garcia, Sharon, Pat Panagoulias, Sam Gurnoe, Conrad Balfour, and Jaune Quick-to-See Smith. DRINK THE WINDS, LET THE WATERS FLOW FREE. Minneapolis: Johnson Institute, 1983. 40 pp.

Brief compilation of American Indian writings (both historical and contemporary) dealing with alcohol and drug abuse, recovery, Indian cultural experience, and spirituality. Includes illustrations.

275. Dobbie, Judy. SUBSTANCE ABUSE AMONG THE ELDERLY. Toronto: Addiction Research Foundation, 1978. 17 pp.

Examines the problems of abuse of alcohol and prescription drugs by the elderly. Discusses the difficulty in distinguishing substance abuse from other problems of aging such as senility or chronic brain syndrome and identifies some of the factors that may contribute to substance abuse.

276. Hamer, John, and Jack Steinbring, eds. ALCOHOL AND NATIVE PEOPLES OF THE NORTH. Lanham, Md.: University Press of America, 1980. 315 pp.

Extensive discussion of contemporary drinking practices among several Canadian Indian tribes, identifying differences as well as similarities in drinking behaviors. Discusses both the negative and positive consequences of Indian alcohol use and examines those factors that seem to have the greatest effect on a tribe's ability to cope with alcohol use. Identifies the institutions that generally deal with alcohol problems (particularly the jailhouse) and offers suggestions for dealing more successfully with these issues.

277. Harper, Frederick D. ALCOHOL AND BLACKS: AN OVERVIEW. Alexandria, Va.: Douglass Publishers, 1976. 20 pp.

Summarizes basic knowledge about drinking practices of Blacks and discusses how these differ from White drinking patterns. Offers suggestions to aid in prevention and treatment of alcohol problems among Blacks.

278. Harper, Frederick D., ed. ALCOHOL ABUSE AND BLACK AMERICA. Alexandria, Va.: Douglass Publishers, 1976. 229 pp.

Presents an overview of alcohol use and alcohol problems among Blacks in the United States, including chapters on specific segments of the Black population (urban Blacks, rural Blacks, women, adolescents). The focus is on Black drinking problems--physiological problems, crime, family disruption. Several chapters are devoted to training alcohol counselors and other treatment personnel. There are also helpful appendixes, including a glossary of terms, a bibliography, further resources for funding or information, and a list of organizations dealing with Black alcoholics.

279. Hazelden Foundation. THE HOMOSEXUAL ALCOHOLIC: AA'S MESSAGE OF HOPE TO GAY MEN AND WOMEN. Center City, Minn.: Hazelden, 1980. 13 pp.

Description of the special problems suffered by homosexuals who are also alcoholics (a "minority inside a minority"). Discusses the benefits of A.A. groups for gays and answers several commonly asked questions about these groups and about gay alcoholism.

280. Johnson Institute. SOBER DAYS, GOLDEN YEARS: ALCOHOLISM AND THE OLDER PERSON. Minneapolis: Johnson Institute, 1981. 43 pp.

Booklet provides a summary of alcohol use and alcohol problems (including the use of alcohol with other drugs) by and among the elderly. A brief look at programs and organizations for help is followed by a more detailed list of recovery resources across the nation for elderly alcoholics.

281. Kelso, Dianne R., and Carolyn L. Attneave. BIBLIOGRAPHY OF NORTH AMERICAN INDIAN MENTAL HEALTH. Westport, Conn.: Greenwood Press, 1981. 411 pp.

Listing of over 1300 references to published and unpublished research studies on all aspects of American Indian mental health. Includes approximately 225 references to research on alcohol use. Items are arranged by accession number and must be located by use of a glossary and a descriptor index. Entries include author, title, date, publication information, a list of subject descriptors (index terms), and identifiers such as institutions or programs that provide additional information about the research. In addition to the descriptor index, items may be located through the culture area and tribe list.

282. McGee, Gloria, and Leola Johnson with Peter Bell. BLACK, BEAUTIFUL AND RECOVERING. Center City, Minn.: Hazelden, 1985. 11 pp.

Discusses some of the special needs and concerns of Black men and women who are recovering from alcohol or other drug abuse. Focuses on issues of Black identity that can inhibit recovery, such as poor self-concept, negative stereotypes, and racially based role expectations. Identifies several tools that can aid in achieving sobriety, including the church, the family, treatment centers, and recovery programs like Alcoholics Anonymous.

283. Mail, Patricia D., and David R. McDonald. TULAPAI TO TOKAY: A BIBLIOGRAPHY OF ALCOHOL USE AND ABUSE AMONG NATIVE AMERICANS OF NORTH AMERICA. New Haven, Conn.: Human Relations Area Files Press, 1981. 372 pp.

Lists nearly 1000 items dating from 1900-1977 dealing with any aspect of Native American alcohol use in North America. Includes published materials (books, book chapters, journal articles) as well as unpublished papers, reports, and theses. Entries are annotated and arranged by author; content evaluations are not included. The bibliography is prefaced by a lengthy review of the literature, and subject and author indexes are provided. Suitable for researchers or laypersons concerned with alcohol use or alcohol problems among American Indians.

284. Michael, John. THE GAY DRINKING PROBLEM...THERE IS A SOLUTION. Minneapolis, CompCare Publications, 1976. 15 pp.

Briefly describes the lifestyle and problems of homosexuals who become alcoholic. Outlines the symptoms of a developing drinking problem and suggests resources for help, such as Alcoholics Anonymous or Alcoholics Together.

285. Michael, John. SOBER, CLEAN AND GAY! Minneapolis: CompCare Publications, 1977. 19 pp.

Discusses the problems of sobriety as they relate to recovering homosexual alcoholics. Emphasizes the importance of support groups such as Alcoholics Anonymous, Alcoholics Together, and Gay Alcoholics Anonymous, which call for honesty, acceptance of one's condition, and submission to a higher power.

286. Mishara, Brian L., and Robert Kastenbaum. ALCOHOL AND OLD AGE. New York: Grune and Stratton, 1980. 220 pp.

Examines drinking patterns and problems among the elderly. Includes a historical overview of alcohol use, a chemical breakdown of alcoholic beverages, and a look at the physiological effects of alcohol use (with a comparison of the different effects on the young and the old). Also contains a chapter on the possible beneficial effects of alcohol use by the elderly.

287. National Institute on Aging. AGING AND ALCOHOL. Washington, D.C.: U.S. Government Printing Office, 1981. 2 pp.

Describes briefly the varied nature and prevalence of alcohol-related problems among the elderly. Emphasizes the physiological and emotional changes that are part of the aging process and discusses their relationship to alcohol use. Offers suggestions for preventing alcohol abuse among this target group.

288. National Institute on Alcohol Abuse and Alcoholism. THE UNSEEN CRISIS: BLACKS AND ALCOHOL. Washington, D.C.: U.S. Government Printing Office, 1977. 13 pp.

Briefly discusses the dangers of alcohol abuse among Blacks and suggests ways in which individuals and community organizations can help in preventing and dealing with alcohol problems.

289. National Institute on Drug Abuse. BIBLIOGRAPHY ON MULTICULTURAL DRUG ABUSE PREVENTION ISSUES. Compiled by Center for Multicultural Awareness. Washington, D.C.: U.S. Government Printing Office, 1981. 64 pp.

Lists a large number of printed materials (books, articles, pamphlets, government reports, unpublished papers) dealing with the prevention of drug and alcohol problems in ethnic communities in the United States. Entries are arranged by author within four broad categories: primary prevention for multicultural communities, bicultural women and substance abuse, program processes for planning and implementing multicultural prevention programs, and Spanish and bilingual materials on drug abuse prevention. Although the focus is on drug abuse, there are a number of titles that include alcohol as a drug or specifically deal with alcohol problems. Each entry includes full citation plus name and address of the source for obtaining the item. The bibliography contains materials for students, the general public, researchers, professsional and non-professional alcohol workers and social service personnel, but there are no content descriptions or indicators of audience level.

290. Nebraska. Division on Alcoholism and Drug Abuse. ELDERLY AND ALCOHOL. Alcohol Effects Series. Lincoln: Nebraska Alcohol and Drug Information Clearinghouse, n.d. 3 pp.

Provides brief descriptions of the physiological effects of alcohol use by the elderly and emphasizes the dangers of multi-drug use with alcohol.

291. Szapocznik, Jose, ed. MENTAL HEALTH, DRUG AND ALCOHOL ABUSE: AN HISPANIC ASSESSMENT OF PRESENT AND FUTURE CHALLENGES. Washington, D.C.: National Coalition of Hispanic Mental Health and Human Services Organizations, 1979. 82 pp.

Discussion of the difficulties in service delivery to Hispanics for alcohol, drug, and mental health problems. Focuses on cultural barriers in the utilization of traditional service programs and offers suggestions for developing culturally oriented treatment and prevention programs for Hispanics in the community and in the workplace.

292. Trachtman, Lester N. ALCOHOLISM, THE OLDER WORKER AND RETIREMENT. New York: Central Labor Rehabilitation Council of New York, 1983. 23 pp.

Describes the nature and scope of alcohol problems among the elderly, focusing especially on problems related to retirement. Includes guidelines for dealing with the problems of elderly employees at the workplace and offers suggestions for organizing a retirement planning program.

293. Trotter, Robert T., II, and Juan Antonio Chavira. EL USO DE ALCOHOL: A RESOURCE BOOK FOR SPANISH SPEAKING COMMUNITIES. Atlanta, Ga.: Southern Area Alcohol Education and Training Program, 1977. 100 pp.

Compendium brings together and analyzes published and unpublished materials dealing with alcohol use among

Spanish-speaking communities in the United States and Latin America. Contains annotated bibliographies of printed works (books, journal articles, government documents, unpublished papers) on cross-cultural studies of alcohol use, alcohol use in Latin America, and alcohol use among Hispanics in the United States. Also includes an annotated resource list of print and non-print materials for alcohol education and prevention among Hispanics. In addition there is a section of original articles dealing with special treatment needs and programs for Hispanics. This manual would serve as a helpful resource for researchers, educators, treatment personnel, and community and social service workers.

294. Twerski, Abraham J. IT HAPPENS TO DOCTORS, TOO. Center City, Minn.: Hazelden, 1982. 154 pp.

Discusses the problems of alcohol and drug addiction among physicians and nurses. Describes the major factors leading to addiction with particular focus on the psychological needs and stresses of persons in the health professions. Includes suggestions for identifying and getting help for impaired professionals.

295. Waddell, Jack O., and Michael W. Everett, eds. DRINKING BEHAVIOR AMONG SOUTHWESTERN INDIANS: AN ANTHROPOLOGICAL PERSPECTIVE. Tucson: University of Arizona Press, 1980. 248 pp.

Ethnographic studies of the drinking behaviors of four southwestern Indian populations; offers insights for more effective treatment programs to deal with Indian alcohol problems. Focuses on the cultural aspects of many Indian drinking practices and stresses the need to consider these aspects when planning Indian treatment programs. Includes discussion by Indian researchers and alcohol program personnel as well as non-Indian anthropologists.

296. Walker, Bobby, and Phil Kelly. THE ELDERLY: A GUIDE FOR COUNSELORS. Professional Education Series, No. 1. Center City, Minn.: Hazelden, 1981. 18 pp.

Discusses the process of aging and the special problems encountered by elderly alcohol abusers. Suggests needs and issues to consider and techniques to use when counseling elderly alcoholics.

297. Watts, Thomas D., and Roosevelt Wright, Jr. eds. BLACK ALCOHOLISM: TOWARD A COMPREHENSIVE UNDERSTANDING. Springfield, Ill.: Charles C. Thomas, 1983. 242 pp.

Presents an overview of research on various aspects of alcohol use and abuse among Black Americans. Looks at the incidence and contributing factors of Black alcoholism and discusses the effectiveness of different treatment approaches for dealing with Black alcohol problems. Also examines several models and strategies for preventing alcohol-related problems among Blacks and offers recommendations for future research and policy directions. The appendix is divided into separate lists of resources to contact for more information about alcohol problems among a variety of ethnic groups: Blacks, Hispanics, Native Americans, Asian Americans, and Jews. Intended for researchers, alcohol professionals, health or social service providers, and concerned laypersons.

298. Yurman, Joanne. OLDER PEOPLE AND ALCOHOLISM. New York: National Council on Alcoholism, 1983. 8 pp.

Briefly outlines some possible problems that may result from excessive alcohol use by older persons. Describes nine groups of symptoms (such as psychological dependence on alcohol and problems with family and friends due to alcohol use) that indicate a developing drinking problem and suggests several resources for help. Also offers some alternatives to alcohol use for the elderly, including volunteer activities, exercise, and education about alcohol and other drugs.

See also: 21, 89, 202, 339

12. ALCOHOL AND THE FETUS

Over the past decade researchers have clearly defined a set of physical and intellectual impairments in a number of children born to alcoholic mothers. These symptoms are collectively known as the fetal alcohol syndrome (FAS). The materials in this section deal with the risks of drinking during pregnancy, focusing primarily on FAS. Most items are written for pregnant women or women who are considering motherhood. A few items are appropriate for social service workers or health care personnel.

299. Addiction Research Foundation. CAN I TAKE THIS IF I'M PREGNANT? Toronto: Addiction Research Foundation, 1979. 6 pp.

Provides brief information about the use of alcohol and other social and non-prescription drugs during pregnancy. Includes such drugs as analgesics, laxatives, antihistamines, caffeine, tobacco, and cannabis. Cautions against alcohol use by expectant mothers.

300. Blume, Sheila B. DRINKING AND PREGNANCY: PREVENTING FETAL ALCOHOL SYNDROME. Minneapolis: Johnson Institute, 1981. 20 pp.

Describes the physical and mental effects of fetal alcohol syndrome (damage to the fetus caused by the mother's alcohol use). Provides guidelines on alcohol use for pregnant women as well as suggestions to help physicians identify alcohol problems among female patients.

301. Dobbie, Judy, and Philippa Bill. FETAL ALCOHOL SYNDROME. Toronto: Addiction Research Foundation, 1978. 11 pp.

Describes research in the early 1970s that confirmed the existence of the fetal alcohol syndrome (FAS). Identifies the symptoms of FAS and relates the syndrome to the drinking habits of the mother.

302. Hafen, Brent Q., and Kathyrn J. Frandsen. FETAL ALCOHOL SYNDROME. Center City, Minn.: Hazelden, 1980. 18 pp.

Explains the effects of alcohol on the developing fetus and emphasizes the risk of mental and physical damage to the newborn whose mother drinks heavily. Describes in some detail the symptoms of fetal alcohol syndrome, including mental retardation, growth deficiencies, facial malformations, and heart problems.

303. March of Dimes Birth Defects Foundation. DRUGS ALCOHOL TOBACCO ABUSE DURING PREGNANCY (DATA). White Plains, N.Y.: March of Dimes Birth Defects Foundation, 1979. 2pp.

Describes briefly the effects that various drugs taken during pregnancy can have on the developing fetus. Includes alcohol, tobacco, street drugs, prescription drugs, and over-the-counter medications.

304. March of Dimes Birth Defects Foundation. PREGNANT? BEFORE YOU DRINK, THINK.... White Plains, N.Y.: March of Dimes Birth Defects Foundation, 1983. 2 pp.

Briefly discusses how drinking to excess during pregnancy can damage an unborn child. Includes a description of the symptoms of fetal alcohol syndrome--a group of physical and mental defects attributed to the mother's alcohol use.

305. National Council on Alcoholism. WHAT YOU NEED TO KNOW ABOUT YOU, YOUR BABY, AND DRINKING. New York: National Council on Alcoholism, 1978. 3 pp.

Designed to caution pregnant teenagers about the effects of alcohol on the fetus. Includes basic information on alcohol as well as the effects of smoking and diet during pregnancy.

306. National Institute on Alcohol Abuse and Alcoholism. ALCOHOL AND YOUR UNBORN BABY. Prepared by Marian Sandmaier. Washington, D.C.: U.S. Government Printing Office, 1978. 14 pp.

Describes the risks of heavy drinking by expectant mothers on the normal development of the unborn baby. Fetal alcohol syndrome and related health consequences--premature birth, low birth weight, small head size, mental retardation, and birth defects--for newborns are identified, and their relationship to maternal alcohol use (in moderate and heavy doses) is discussed.

307. National Institute on Alcohol Abuse and Alcoholism. SHOULD I DRINK? Rockville, Md.: National Clearinghouse for Alcohol Information, 1980. 4 pp.

Uses photographs and drawings to illustrate the possible effects of alcohol use by pregnant women on the developing fetus. Lists the symptoms and consequences of fetal alcohol syndrome and offers guidelines on reducing risks to the unborn child.

308. Nebraska. Division on Alcoholism and Drug Abuse. FETAL ALCOHOL EFFECTS. Alcohol Effects Series. Lincoln: Nebraska Alcohol and Drug Information Clearinghouse, n.d. 3 pp.

Description of the birth defects, including physical defects and mental retardation, which may result from alcohol use by pregnant women.

309. Robe, Lucy B. ALCOHOL AND PREGNANCY: WHY THEY DON'T MIX. Chicago: American Medical Association, 1984. 13 pp.

Outlines the physiological damage that alcohol can cause to an unborn baby. Describes the symptoms of fetal alcohol syndrome and fetal alcohol effects (including mental and growth retardation and facial abnormalities) and discusses levels of alcohol use and their attendant risks for expectant mothers.

310. Robe, Lucy B. JUST SO IT'S HEALTHY. rev. ed. Minneapolis: CompCare Publications, 1982. 165 pp.

Discusses the dangers to the unborn baby of alcohol and drug use by expectant mothers. Part one deals with alcohol use, focusing particularly on the risk of developing fetal alcohol syndrome (FAS). Part two deals with other drugs, including popular prescription drugs (antibiotics, antihistamines, hormones), over-the-counter drugs, and mood-altering drugs (narcotics, tranquilizers, marijuana). There is also a section on caffeine, cigarettes, and artificial sweeteners. A lengthy bibliography and a helpful chart to record drugs taken during pregnancy are included.

311. U.S. Bureau of Alcohol, Tobacco and Firearms. REX MORGAN, M.D., TALKS ABOUT YOUR UNBORN CHILD! Rockville, Md.: National Clearinghouse for Alcohol Information, 1980. 14 pp.

Booklet presents information in comic-book format about drinking during pregnancy. Discusses how even moderate drinking may be damaging to the fetus and offers advice to promote healthy fetal development.

See also: 208, 209, 211, 401.

13. ALCOHOL PROBLEMS IN INDUSTRY

According to the federal government, alcohol-impaired workers cost billions of dollars each year in lost productivity, absenteeism, industrial accidents, and health care expenditures. More and more employers are realizing the impact of these losses and are offering programs to identify and help troubled employees. Materials in this section deal with the prevalence and consequences of alcohol problems in the workplace. Many of the entries focus on employee assistance programs (EAPs) designed to help workers with personal problems--particularly alcoholism--that affect job performance.

312. Association of Labor-Management Administrators and Consultants on Alcoholism. RESOURCE INFORMATION ON EMPLOYEE ALCOHOLISM/ASSISTANCE PROGRAMS. Arlington, Va.: Association of Labor-Management Administrators and Consultants on Alcoholism, 1983. 19 pp.

Provides useful information for companies or unions that want to start an employee assistance program (EAP) to help employees with alcoholism or other personal problems that are affecting job performance. The booklet contains a list of program standards covering policy and procedures, administrative functions, education and training, resources, and evaluation. There is also a resource list of organizations for further help, an annotated list of books (with publishers' addresses) dealing with EAPs, and a brief list of relevant journals and newsletters (two of which, however, are no longer being published).

313. Association of Labor-Management Administrators and Consultants on Alcoholism. STANDARDS FOR EMPLOYEE ALCOHOLISM AND/OR ASSISTANCE PROGRAMS. Arlington, Va.: Association of Labor-Management Administrators and Consultants on Alcoholism, n.d. 6 pp.

Concise set of guidelines for designing an effective employee assistance program to help employees with alcohol, drug, or other problems that are hurting job performance.

314. Blair, Brenda R. ALCOHOLISM AND DRUG DEPENDENCY: THE SUPERVISOR'S ROLE IN EARLY RECOVERY. Minneapolis: Johnson Institute, 1984. 27 pp.

Presents helpful guidelines for supervisors dealing with newly recovered alcoholic employees. Emphasizes the importance of involving supervisors in the recovery process and discusses realistic expectations regarding the employee's job performance.

315. Blair, Brenda R. SUPERVISORS AND MANAGERS AS ENABLERS. Minneapolis: Johnson Institute, 1983. 20 pp.

Description of the role inadvertently played by supervisors regarding alcoholic employees. Discusses a supervisor's emotional reactions toward an alcoholic employee's behavior and job performance and offers examples of how the supervisor's actions may prevent the employee from experiencing the full effects of his problem. Provides suggestions for help for enablers in the workplace.

316. Brisolara, Ashton. THE ALCOHOLIC EMPLOYEE: A HANDBOOK OF USEFUL GUIDELINES. New York: Human Sciences Press, 1979. 168 pp.

Examines the problems caused by alcohol and drug abusing workers (including symptoms of a developing problem) and offers practical quidelines for establishing a company program to deal with these problems. Provides basic information about the physiological and behavioral effects of alcohol and other drug use. Outlines a company program based on documentation of declining work performance, diagnosis of problem, and referral to appropriate agency. The basic elements of the program--policy, supervisory training, and referral--are described in some detail, and several case histories are provided to illustrate how such a program works.

317. Carter, Elliott E. THE OBSTACLE COURSE: A GUIDE TO VOCATIONAL RECOVERY. 2d ed. Stratford, N.J.: The

Obstacle Course, 1981. 142 pp.

Offers practical suggestions to help recovering alcoholics find employment. Includes tips on filling out job applications, resume enhancing, and minimizing a poor medical or work history. Also covers interviewing strategies and presents helpful (often amusing) examples of job-seeking situations.

318. Dunkin, William S. THE EAP MANUAL: A PRACTICAL, STEP-BY-STEP GUIDE TO ESTABLISHING AN EFFECTIVE EMPLOYEE ALCOHOLISM/ASSISTANCE PROGRAM. New York: National Council on Alcoholism, 1982. 91 pp.

Discusses the concept of employee assistance programs to identify alcoholic employees and motivate them to accept treatment. Outlines the key elements in a program, including a company alcoholism policy, referral system, supervisory training, the role of organized labor, record keeping, and insurance coverage. Includes sample policies and procedures, record-keeping forms, and resource lists.

319. EMPLOYEE ASSISTANCE PROGRAMS: THEORY AND OPERATION. Pittsburgh, Pa.: Aluminum Company of America, Corporate Employee Assistance Program, n.d. 12 pp.

Discusses some of the various personal problems (including alcoholism) that can affect an employee's work performance and demonstrates how these can be handled by an employee assistance program (EAP). Explains the theory and basic components of an EAP and presents examples to show how the program works. Includes a list of standards or guidelines covering policy and procedures, administrative functions, education and training, resources, and evaluation to help companies that wish to start an EAP.

320. Follman, Joseph F., Jr. ALCOHOLICS AND BUSINESS: PROBLEMS, COSTS, SOLUTIONS. New York: Amacom, 1976. 246 pp.

Outlines the economic costs of alcoholism to business due to high rates of absenteeism, disability, accidents, illness, and premature deaths. Provides guidelines for establishing a company alcoholism program and presents examples of recovery rates and cost-savings from such programs.

321. Harrison, Earl. BOOZLEBANE ON ALCOHOLISM AND WORK. Center City, Minn.: Hazelden, 1984. 14 pp.

Tongue-in-cheek spoof illustrating the different effects of alcoholism on the workplace. Focuses on the use of denial by employees and supervisors and also discusses the feelings of shame, inadequacy, and resentment experienced by alcoholics and their colleagues on the job.

322. Hazelden Foundation. ALCOHOL AND DRUG PROBLEMS: YOUR EMPLOYEE ASSISTANCE PROGRAM. Center City, Minn.: Hazelden, 1978. 2 pp.

Briefly describes problems related to drug and alcohol abuse and explains how a company employee assistance program can help. This leaflet is part of a series that describes problems that can be helped through an employee assistance program. Other leaflets deal with such topics as stress and family problems. The series can be used by companies to acquaint employees with an existing or newly implemented program.

323. Jones, Donald. PERFORMANCE BENCHMARKS FOR THE COMPREHENSIVE EMPLOYEE ASSISTANCE PROGRAM. Center City, Minn.: Hazelden, 1983. 49 pp.

Discusses the importance of evaluating employee assistance programs (dealing with alcohol, drug, and other personal problems of employees) in order to justify their continuation and expansion. Uses data from the Hazelden Employee Assistance Program to illustrate the most important outcome measures, such as program utilization rates, supervisor participation, family participation, referral rates (to other treatment resources), and job performance. Also suggests "benchmarks" (criteria) for evaluating any employee assistance program.

324. Milstead, Robin J. EMPOWERING WOMEN ALCOHOLICS TO HELP THEMSELVES AND THEIR SISTERS IN THE WORKPLACE. Dubuque, Iowa: Kendall/Hunt, 1981. 191 pp.

Deals with the problems of employed women alcoholics and suggests an alternative occupational program geared specifically toward their needs. The program, called EMPOWER (Employee Managed Program on Women Employees' Recovery), combines elements of traditional occupational programming with existing community services and components of the Women for Sobriety program (a self-help program for women alcoholics).

325. Moree, Gerald B., and Robert J. Jernigan. TREAT ALCOHOLIC WORKERS AND STOP THE DOLLAR DRAIN. Minneapolis: CompCare Publications, 1977. 22 pp.

Describes the warning signs and stages of alcoholism and how this disease can affect an employee's work performance. Discusses the underlying concepts of an employee alcoholism program and outlines the steps a supervisor can follow to confront a troubled employee on the basis of poor job performance.

326. Muldoon, Joseph A., and Mitchell Berdie. EFFECTIVE EMPLOYEE ASSISTANCE: A COMPREHENSIVE GUIDE FOR THE EMPLOYER. rev. ed. Minneapolis: CompCare Publications, 1980. 151 pp.

Provides step-by-step guidelines for the planning and implementation of a program to deal with a wide range of employee personal problems (such as alcohol or drug abuse, family problems, financial or legal difficulties). Offers suggestions for conducting a needs assessment, writing a successful proposal, training supervisory personnel, publicizing and evaluating the program. Includes sample policies and procedures, data collection forms, a cost-benefit analysis, and resource lists of materials and organizations for assistance.

327. National Institute on Alcohol Abuse and Alcoholism. TARGET: ALCOHOL ABUSE IN THE HARD-TO-REACH WORK FORCE; IDEAS AND RESOURCES FOR RESPONDING TO PROBLEMS OF THE HARD-TO-REACH WORK FORCE. Rockville, Md.: National Clearinghouse for Alcohol Information, 1982. 27 pp.

Focuses on the need for alcoholism programs for workers who are not served by traditional employee alcoholism programs. Includes in this group all workers who are not regularly under direct supervision, such as the self-employed or members of large companies with dispersed locations. Suggests a variety of possible approaches to bring alcoholism services to this population, such as consortia (for groups of small businesses), service networks (for dispersed companies), labor union alcoholism programs, and programs established by professioanl associations.

328. Phillips, Donald A., and Deborah J. Milliken. SO THE BOSS HAS A PROBLEM. Center City, Minn.: Hazelden, 1980. 23 pp.

Examines the difficulties experienced by an employee whose boss's problems (family difficulties, financial troubles, alcohol dependency, etc.) are affecting his job performance. Five types of relationships between an employee and his troubled boss are identified, ranging from the employee's unawareness of any problem to his victimization by the boss's unpredictable behavior. Suggestions for counseling employees on how to deal with the boss's behavior, including some guidelines on intervention and confrontation with the boss, are provided.

329. Phillips, Donald A., Arthur J. Purvis, and Harry J. Older. TURNING SUPERVISORS ON (TO EMPLOYEE COUNSELING PROGRAMS). Center City, Minn.: Hazelden, 1980. 38 pp.

Outlines a model for training supervisors to identify and deal effectively with troubled employees--particularly those with alcohol problems. Focuses on the direct link between employee behaviors and the feeling and behavior responses of supervisors. Intended for use within an employee assistance program.

330. Smithers, Christopher D., Foundation. A COMPANY PROGRAM ON ALCOHOLISM: BASIC OUTLINE. Mill Neck, N.Y.: Christopher D. Smithers Foundation, 1974 (8th printing). 42 pp.

Exploration of the changing focus of businesses and industries toward alcoholic employees and describes the basic concepts which underlie company programs on alcoholism. Discusses the key elements of a company program, including policy, rehabilitation facilities, program costs, union participation, and supervisory training.

331. Smithers, Christopher D., Foundation. THE KEY ROLE OF LABOR IN EMPLOYEE ALCOHOLISM PROGRAMS. Mill Neck, N.Y.: Christopher D. Smithers Foundation, n.d. 32 pp.

Examines the importance of involving labor unions in employee alcoholism programs. Discusses the need for cooperation among union officals, supervisors, and management in identifying employees whose job performance or behavior is causing problems. Includes recommendations for a labor-management planning committee to develop a company alcoholism program. There is also a helpful chart which shows the symptoms (including signs on the job) of a developing alcohol problem as well as the stages of recovery.

332. Sorenson, Darrell D. THE ART OF PRESERVING HUMAN RESOURCES. Omaha: National Publications, 1978. 95 pp.

Offers practical suggestions on how to plan and implement an employee assistance program to help workers who have alcohol, drug, family, or other personal problems. Discusses the basic concept of an employee assistance program (to identify and help workers whose problems are affecting their job performance) and includes suggestions on how to sell this concept to management. Explains the roles which management and labor should play in employee assistance programs and provides a detailed outline and discussion on how to plan and start a program, including staffing and utilization of community resources. A helpful glossary of terms (most of which are related to alcohol use) is also included.

333. Spicer, Jerry, Patricia Owen, and David Levine EVALUATING EMPLOYEE ASSISTANCE PROGRAMS: A SOURCEBOOK FOR THE ADMINISTRATOR AND COUNSELOR. Center City, Minn.: Hazelden, 1983. 95 pp.

Provides information on the concepts and methodologies of program evaluation for personnel who work with employee assistance programs (designed to help employees with alcohol, drug, or other personal problems). Discusses the value of program evaluation and includes examples of specific techniques for evaluating program procedures and components as well as client outcome and cost-benefit findings.

334. THE SUPERVISOR'S HANDBOOK ON SUBSTANCE ABUSE. Pompano Beach, Fla.: Health Communications, 1977. 14 pp.

Discussion of the supervisor's important role in identifying and intervening with employees whose alcohol or drug problems are interfering with their jobs. Also includes suggestions for helping rehabilitated employees readjust to the work environment.

335. Trice, Harrison M. ALCOHOLISM IN INDUSTRY: MODERN PROCEDURES. Mill Neck, N.Y.: Christopher D. Smithers Foundation, n.d. 67 pp.

Identifies and discusses the basic elements in a successful employee alcoholism program, including a company alcohol policy, treatment resources (in-house medical or counseling personnel or outside treatment programs), early discovery of the alcoholic employee, and motivating the employee into treatment. There is also a section that offers suggestions for modifying an alcoholism program to work for smaller companies.

336. Winick, Charles. A LABOR APPROACH TO DEALING WITH ALCOHOL PROBLEMS AT THE WORK PLACE. New York: Central Labor Rehabilitation Council of New York, 1982. 23 pp.

Presents the concepts, goals, and procedures for establishing a union-based employee assistance program to help employees troubled by alcohol, drugs, or other personal problems. Points out some advantages of having a union or joint union-management program, especially for employees in small companies or those whose employment changes frequently (maritime and construction workers, etc.). Describes the most common program components and procedures.

337. Wrich, James T. THE EMPLOYEE ASSISTANCE PROGRAM UPDATED FOR THE 1980'S. Center City, Minn.: Hazelden, 1980. 249 pp.

Description of the basic concept behind employee assistance programming--identifying employees with problems (alcohol or drug abuse, family problems, financial difficulties, etc.) in order to successfully treat them without job loss. Guidelines for implementing a new program, sample company policies, cost and insurance factors, and evaluation techniques are included. There are also sample program materials (flyers, client assessment forms) and a helpful directory of further resources.

See also: 21, 89, 215, 221, 292.

14. ALCOHOL AND TRAFFIC SAFETY

The growth of citizen-activist groups (such as Mothers Against Drunk Drivers) that advocate stricter drunk driving legislation has brought the isssue of alcohol and highway safety more visibly to public attention. Materials in this chapter cover the nature, prevalence, and prevention of drunk driving problems. Most are designed for use by citizens groups, parents, teenagers, or educators.

338. ABC'S OF DRINKING AND DRIVING: FACTS ABOUT AMERICA'S NO. 1 SAFETY PROBLEM. rev. ed. South Deerfield, Mass.: Channing L. Bete Co., 1983. 15 pp.

Presents information about alcohol consumption in the United States and alcohol involvement in traffic accidents. Explains the meaning of blood alcohol concentration and relates this to drinking and driving legislation.

339. American Automobile Association Foundation for Traffic Safety. SENIOR ADULTS, TRAFFIC SAFETY AND ALCOHOL. Falls Church, Va.: AAA Foundation for Traffic Safety, n.d. 7 pp.

Briefly discusses the involvement of alcohol in traffic accidents with elderly persons. Outlines the effects of alcohol on the brain and on skills needed for driving and offers suggestions to avoid the risk of drinking and driving.

340. DRUNK DRIVING: A KILLER WE CAN STOP. New York: Insurance Information Institute, 1983. 11 pp.

Suggests actions for concerned citizens to pursue in the fight against drunk driving. Includes names and addresses of volunteer organizations and other sources of information.

341. DRUNK DRIVING: WHAT CAN I DO? A SENSIBLE LOOK AT THE DRUNK DRIVING PROBLEM. Washington, D.C.: Health Education Foundation, 1983. 10 pp.

Examines the various common attitudes toward drunk driving and discusses the effectiveness of legal and social approaches to combat the problem. Offers practical suggestions, including guidelines to follow when serving alcohol at a party, to help prevent drunk driving.

342. HOW ALCOHOL AND DRUGS AFFECT YOUR DRIVING SKILLS. South Deerfield, Mass.: Channing L. Bete Co., 1984. 15 pp.

Describes the effects of alcohol and other drugs on driving ability. Discusses reaction time, judgment, muscle coordination, visual impairment, and loss of concentration. Includes effects of alcohol, antihistamines, tranquilizers, stimulants, marijuana, and other pain relievers and also discusses the dangers of mixing alcohol with other drugs. Practical suggestions for avoiding drunk driving situations are offered.

343. Mann, Peggy. ARRIVE ALIVE: HOW TO KEEP DRUNK AND POT-HIGH DRIVERS OFF THE HIGHWAY. New York: Woodmere Press, 1983. 349 pp.

Presents statistics on the costs in lives and dollars of alcohol-related traffic accidents and offers suggestions for preventing drunk driving. Contains information about the physiological effects of alcohol and marijuana on driving ability. Describes a variety of prevention approaches, including media spots, organized pressure for stronger legislation, and public education campaigns to alert citizens to the dangers of alcohol or marijuana use and driving. The work of groups such as Mothers Against Drunk Drivers (MADD) and Remove Intoxicated Drivers (RID) is covered.

344. National Highway Traffic Safety Administration. AN ACTIVIST'S GUIDE FOR CURBING THE DRUNK DRIVER. Washington, D.C.: U.S. Government Printing Office, 1977. 20 pp.

Presents information about the effects of alcohol on driving ability. Outlines specific steps for preventing people who plan to drive from becoming intoxicated and for people who plan to drive from becoming intoxicated and for keeping those who have drunk too much off the road. Also offers suggestions for various groups (friends, parents, employers and employees, law enforcement personnel) to help promote more responsible attitudes toward drinking and driving.

345. National Highway Traffic Safety Administration. HOW MUCH DO YOU KNOW ABOUT DRINKING AND DRIVING? A SELF EVALUATION FOR TEENAGERS. Washington, D.C.: U.S. Government Printing Office, 1983. 16 pp.

Booklet presents forty statements to test teenagers' attitudes and perceptions about the effects of alcohol use on driving skills as well as the relationships between alcohol use, peer pressure, and adult pressure. Contains instructions for plotting an individual profile and comparing with national results. Also includes a short knowledge test focusing on alcohol intoxication and its effects on driving.

346. National Highway Traffic Safety Administration. HOW TO SAVE LIVES AND REDUCE INJURIES: A CITIZEN ACTIVIST GUIDE TO EFFECTIVELY FIGHT DRUNK DRIVING. Washington, D.C.: U.S. Government Printing Office, 1982. 131 pp.

Provides guidelines for grassroots organizing against drunk drivers. Includes suggestions for developing citizen activist groups and task forces to lobby for better drunk driving legislation. Discusses the role of the police and the court system in enforcing drunk driving laws and offers tips on using the media to increase public awareness of the drunk driving problem. Contains a number of helpful appendixes, including a list of citizen activist groups, sample task force letters, press releases, and news articles.

347. National Institute on Alcohol Abuse and Alcoholism. THE SECRETARY'S CONFERENCE FOR YOUTH ON DRINKING AND DRIVING. Washington, D.C.: U.S. Government Printing Office, 1983. 67 pp. plus appendixes.

Reports on the chief underlying concepts and results of a federally sponsored conference on the problems of drinking and driving by youth. Outlines the planning and preparation of materials and presentations for the conference nation-wide) dealing with drinking and driving, as well as other alcohol problems, among youth.

348. National Institute on Alcohol Abuse and Alcoholism. TALKING TO YOUR TEENAGER ABOUT DRINKING AND DRIVING. Rockville, Md.: National Clearinghouse for Alcohol Information, 1981. 7 pp.

Suggests ways that parents can approach their teenage children on the subject of alcohol use and driving. Includes facts about the effects of alcohol on the body and the possible consequences of drunk driving.

349. National Institute on Drug Abuse. DRUGS AND DRIVING. Rockville, Md.: National Clearinghouse for Drug Abuse Information, 1979. 2 pp.

Summarizes the effects of alcohol and other drugs on driving performance. Also warns against mixing alcohol with other drug use.

350. Ross, H. Laurence. DETERRING THE DRINKING DRIVER: LEGAL POLICY AND SOCIAL CONTROL. Lexington, Mass.: Lexington Books, 1982. 129 pp.

Summarizes research on the relationship between alcohol use and traffic accidents and reviews legal deterrents employed by a variety of countries (including the United States) to curb drinking and driving. Evaluates the effectiveness of these deterrents and offers recommendations for future policy development. Useful for decision makers in the area of public safety.

351. Wagenaar, Alexander C. ALCOHOL, YOUNG DRIVERS, AND TRAFFIC ACCIDENTS: EFFECTS OF MINIMUM-AGE LAWS. Lexington, Mass.: Lexington Books, 1983. 151 pp.

Discusses research on alcohol availability, minimum legal drinking age, and traffic accidents involving young people. Includes lengthy bibliography and numerous charts and tables with statistics on drinking age and crash involvement, property damage, and arrests, as well as changes in alcohol sales and distribution. Offers suggestions for development of public policy to reduce alcohol-related problems among youth.

352. Wagenaar, Alexander C. DRINKING AND DRIVING: NEW DIRECTIONS. Minneapolis: Johnson Institute, 1983. 24 pp.

Summarizes the most familiar traditional approaches to reduce alcohol-related traffic accidents, including arrest and punishment of drunk driving offenders, treatment and rehabilitation of offenders, and education campaigns to increase public awareness of the dangers of drinking and driving. Discusses the limited effectiveness of these approaches and suggests alternatives based on limiting alcohol availability (raising the drinking age, raising prices, "dram shop" laws, etc.).

353. WHAT YOUNG ADULTS SHOULD KNOW ABOUT ALCOHOL AND DRIVING. South Deerfield, Mass.: Channing L. Bete Co., 1985. 15 pp.

Describes the effects of alcohol on those behavioral skills necessary for driving (motor coordination, vision, judgement, concentration). Discusses the risks and consequences of driving under the influence of alcohol and offers practical suggestions to avoid drunk driving or to prevent a friend from drinking and driving.

354. Zola, John, Richard Callahan, and Tessa Davis. ALCOHOL, DRUGS, DRIVING AND YOU. Boulder, Colo.: The Prevention Center, 1984. 151 pp. (teacher's manual) plus 65 pp. (student manual).

Curriculum guide designed for use in high school health, driver education, or other related classes. Materials include teacher manual with class outlines, suggested activities, and resource lists, as well as several posters and a student manual. Provides information about the effects of alcohol and other drugs on driving skill and the legal and economic consequences of drunk driving. Uses role play and class discussion to explore alternatives to drinking and driving or riding with an intoxicated driver.

See also: 59, 388.

15. ALCOHOL EDUCATION AND PREVENTION

Prevention of alcohol problems, especialy among youth, has received an increasing amount of attention over the past few years. The federal government has recently funded a National Prevention Center to conduct research into the most effective prevention approaches. Education about alcohol and its effects is a basic component in many prevention efforts. This chapter includes curriculum guides and other teaching materials for use with elementary, secondary, and college students. There are also items for use by clergy, community groups, and social service agencies.

355. ABOUT ALCOHOL AND DRUGS: A COLORING AND ACTIVITIES BOOK. South Deerfield, Mass.: Channing L. Bete Co., 1981. 16 pp

Uses a coloring-book format to present information for elementary school-aged children on alcohol and drugs. Briefly discusses how and why many people use alcohol and drugs and describes some consequences of abuse. Also suggests several activities as alternatives to substance use.

356. ALCOHOL ON AMERICAN CAMPUSES: A DIRECTORY OF PROGRAMS, A SURVEY OF AMERICAN COLLEGES AND A MODEL STUDENT ASSISTANCE ALCOHOL PROGRAM. Policy Perspectives, Vol. 3, No. 3. Newark, N.J.: Policy Perspectives, 1983. 103 pp.

Special issue devoted to alcohol use and abuse on college campuses. Includes example of survey to determine extent of alcohol use and alcohol problems on campus, a listing of alcohol programs (covering education, prevention, and treatment for students and staff), and an analysis of survey findings regarding the number and effectiveness of campus alcohol programs. Also contains an outline of a model student assistance program (with training agenda for personnel and a sample policy statement) for prevention and treatment of alcohol problems.

357. American Business Men's Research Foundation. 8:30 MONDAY MORNING. Lansing, Mich.: American Business Men's Research Foundation, 1977. 250 pp.

Alcohol education curriculum guide for grades 7-12. Explores knowledge about alcohol, attitudes and values regarding alcohol use, and decision-making skills. Includes lesson plans, a booklet on alcohol information, and visual aids. May be used as separate alcohol education units or integrated with other coursework.

358. CASPAR Alcohol Education Project. DECISIONS ABOUT DRINKING. 3d ed. Somerville, Mass.: CASPAR Alcohol Education Project, 1979. varying papes.

Offers a comprehensive alcohol education curriculum to help young people explore values and attitudes toward alcohol use and learn to make responsible decisions about drinking. The curriculum guide is divided into sequential modules with a variety of teaching activities for grades 3-12. In addition there are materials for teacher training and for establishing a peer leader program for high school students.

359. Chemical Use Education Task Force, Lutheran Church in America, Minnesota Synod. CHRISTIAN EDUCATION MATERIALS FOR YOUTH AND FAMILIES: ALCOHOL AND DRUGS. Center City, Minn.: Hazelden, 1983. 54 pp.

Curriculum guide on alcohol and other drugs designed for use in church-sponsored programs. The guide is divided into four lessons and focuses on clarifying values as well as information regarding the responsible use of chemical substances. Lessons include factual information about alcohol and drugs along with topics and stories for discussion, suggestions for related films, and pertinent Bible scriptures regarding alcohol use and intoxication. Stories and films deal with youthful alcohol and drug use and also the problems experienced by children of alcoholic parents.

360. Deutsch, Charles. BROKEN BOTTLES, BROKEN DREAMS: UNDERSTANDING AND HELPING THE CHILDREN OF ALCOHOLICS. New York: Teachers College Press, 1982. 213 pp.

Designed to help the various professionals who work with youth (teachers, counselors, clergy, probation officers, etc.) to recognize and intervene effectively with children who have alcoholic parents. Provides basic information about the disease of alcoholism and discusses in depth the functioning of the alcoholic family and the psychological, emotional, and physiological effects on the children. Offers examples of intervention by various professionals and describes a model prevention program that includes training for professionals and peer education groups.

361. Engs, Ruth C. RESPONSIBLE DRUG AND ALCOHOL USE. New York: Macmillan Publishing Co., 1979. 287 pp.

Focuses on decision making regarding the use of alcohol and other commonly used drugs. Arranged in sections by broad drug classifications (depressants, stimulants, hallucinogens, over-the-counter and common prescription drugs). The chapter on alcohol (a depressant) describes the historical and cultural uses of alcohol, possible causes of alcoholism, and various treatment approaches. Guidelines for responsible drinking behavior are also included. Each chapter begins with a values-clarification exercise to stimulate thinking about drug-related issues. Could be used as a college text.

362. Finn, Peter, and Jane Lawson. ALCOHOL: PLEASURES AND PROBLEMS. New York: National Council on Alcoholism, 1976. 23 pp.

Provides information for teenagers on why people choose to drink or not and how alcohol affects the mind and body. Also discusses drinking and driving, problem drinking, and alcoholism. May be used alone or with the DIAL A-L-C-O-H-O-L film series and teacher's guide (see item no. 364).

363. Finn, Peter, and Jane Lawson. KIDS AND ALCOHOL: FACTS AND IDEAS ABOUT DRINKING AND NOT DRINKING. New York: National Council on Acloholism, 1976. 20 pp.

Designed to accompany the film series JACKSON JUNIOR HIGH and the teacher guide (see item no. 365). Presents information on the physical and behavioral effects of alcohol as well as why kids may choose to drink or not. Briefly discusses some of the signs of problem drinking and offers suggestions for getting help.

364. Finn, Peter, and Jane Lawson. A TEACHER MANUAL FOR USE WITH DIAL A-L-C-O-H-O-L: A FILM SERIES FOR GRADES NINE THROUGH TWELVE ON ALCOHOL EDUCATION. New York: National Council on Alcoholism, 1976. 35 pp.

For use with the film series DIAL A-L-C-O-H-O-L, which focuses on drinking practices and problems of high school students. Contains discussion of the goals of alcohol education, synopsis of the four films, suggested classroom activities, information on the physiological effects of alcohol, and resource lists for teachers and students. Topics covered include peer pressure, parental and social attitudes toward youthful drinking, driving and drinking, and alcoholism. Accompanies student booklet ALCOHOL: PLEASURES AND PROBLEMS (see item no. 362). Originally published by U.S. Department of Health, Education, And Welfare.

365. Finn, Peter, Jane Lawson, Linda Abrams, Karen Tomey, and Michael Ault. A TEACHER MANUAL FOR USE WITH JACKSON JUNIOR HIGH: A FILM SERIES FOR GRADES FIVE THROUGH EIGHT ON ALCOHOL EDUCATION. New York: National Council on Alcoholism, 1976. 35 pp.

Accompanies the film series JACKSON JUNIOR HIGH, which focuses on how and why people use alcoholic beverages and how alcohol affects the body and behavior. Includes synopsis of the films and suggested classroom activities such as discussion and role play. Also designed for use with student booklet KIDS AND ALCOHOL (see item no. 363). Originally published by the U.S. Department of Health, Education, and Welfare.

366. Finn, Peter, and Patricia A. O'Gorman. TEACHING ABOUT ALCOHOL: CONCEPTS, METHODS, AND CLASSROOM ACTIVITIES. Boston: Allyn and Bacon, 1981. 241 pp.

Provides a range of information for elementary through college educators on the goals and objectives of alcohol education, primary prevention of alcohol problems, alcohol use and alcohol problems among youth, and the physiological, behavioral, and social effects of alcohol use. Describes a variety of techniques and approaches for use in the classroom (e.g., role play, group discussion, field trips) and offers suggestions for working with parents and community and for teacher training in alcohol education. Includes guidelines for developing and evaluating an alcohol curriculum unit with samples of instructional activities (games, discussion units, etc.). Additional readings for educators and college students are listed at the end of each chapter. There is also a list of publications and audiovisuals for elementary and secondary students.

367. Gonzalez, Gerardo M. PROCEDURES AND RESOURCE MATERIALS FOR DEVELOPING A CAMPUS ALCOHOL ABUSE PREVENTION PROGRAM: A TESTED MODEL. Gainesville: University of Florida, Alcohol Abuse Prevention Program, 1978. 109 pp.

Presents a step-by-step approach to guidelines for planning and implementing a campus alcohol abuse prevention program, using the University of Florida's program as a model. Includes suggestions for organizing an alcohol awareness conference with a task force to follow through on recommendations. Contains samples of various prevention activities, education courses, training functions, media announcements, and survey instruments, as well as program resources. Also discusses evaluation of a program in terms of effort, process, and effects.

368. Jones, Kenneth L., Louis W. Shainberg, and Curtis O. Byer. DRUGS AND ALCOHOL. 3d ed. New York: Harper and Row, 1979. 214 pp.

College text designed to provide basic information about alcohol and other drugs. Describes commonly abused drugs, effects of drugs on the central nervous system, factors related to drug abuse, and legal issues in drug control. Two chapters are devoted specifically to alcohol use and alcoholism, including such topics as properties of alcoholic beverages, physiological effects of alcohol use, alcohol-related problems (hangovers, drunk driving, etc.), possible causes of alcoholism, and several treatment approaches. Chapter summaries and a helpful glossary of terms are provided.

369. McCarthy, Raymond G. EXPLORING ALCOHOL QUESTIONS. rev. ed. New Brunswick, N.J.: Rutgers Center of Alcohol Studies, 1970. 6 leaflets, 4 pp. each.

Set of six leaflets that provide introductory material on alcohol for junior and senior high school students. Topics covered include American drinking practices and attitudes, metabolism of alcohol in the body, the dangers of drinking and driving, causes and treatment for alcoholism, drinking practices in other parts of the world, and religious and community attitudes toward alcohol use. May be used to supplement other course materials on alcohol, addictions, or public health.

370. Miles, Samuel A., ed. LEARNING ABOUT ALCOHOL: A RESOURCE BOOK FOR TEACHERS. Washington, D.C.: American Association for Health, Physical Education, and Recreation/a national affiliate of the National Education Association, 1974. 168 pp.

Overview of alcohol education designed to help teachers develop effective approaches to the subject. Although not a curriculum guide, it contains a good deal of basic information about alcohol and its use (pharmacology, effects on the body, drinking behaviors and risks, prevalence of use) and emphasizes the importance of individual and social values in determining drinking practices and attitudes. Discusses the principles and objectives of alcohol education and suggests teaching methods and topics for the classroom. The appendix contains a discussion of the manufacture and uses of alcohol, a brief history of health and alcohol education, and lists of print and audiovisual materials about alcohol for teachers and for students.

371. Mills, Kenneth C., Edward M. Neal, and Iola Peed-Neal. HANDBOOK FOR ALCOHOL EDUCATION: THE COMMUNITY APPROACH. Cambridge, Mass.: Ballinger Publishing Co., 1983. 273 pp.

Presentation of the basic steps and components for developing and implementing a community program to solve alcohol-related problems. Focuses on the training of peer educators to assess and seek solutions for community alcohol problems ("problem-specific approach"). Includes information on contemporary drinking practices and problems, techiques for identifying and documenting alcohol problems in the community, guidelines for developing an alcohol policy, basic principles of problem-specific alcohol education, and student work modules to develop facility with various aspects of the alcohol use cycle (drinking behavior, behavioral and biological consequences, attitude formation, etc.)

372. National Center for Alcohol Education. YOU, YOUTH, AND PREVENTION. 3 Vols. Rockville, Md.: National Clearinghouse for Alcohol Information, 1978. varying pages.

Designed to train persons in community-service or alcohol agencies "who are responsible for planning and implementing prevention programs for youth." Materials include trainer manual with session outline cards, participant handbook, and a 16-mm film available for rent from the National Audiovisual Center. There are four training sessions which emphasize communication skills, prevention concepts, and suggestions for selecting and implementing a prevention strategy appropriate to an agency's needs. Addendixes include information on alcohol and annotated lists of resources (organizations, materials, demonstration projects, etc.). Participants should have some background knowledge of alcohol and its effects before starting this program.

373. National Institute on Alcohol Abuse and Alcoholism. ALCOHOL-SPECIFIC CURRICULA: A SELECTED LIST, 1980. Prepared by Mary L. Mong. Washington, D.C.: U.S. Government Printing Office, 1980. 20 pp.

Description of eleven different curricula designed specifically for alcohol education courses at the elementary or secondary school level. Includes target group, description of content, special focus, and ordering information for each item.

374. National Institute on Alcohol Abuse and Alcoholism. IS BEER A FOUR LETTER WORD? Prepared by Keith Hewitt and Mary Hughes. Washington, D.C.: U.S. Goverment Printing Office, 1978. 58 pp.

Presents twelve "Action Plans" designed for use by high school students to help prevent alcohol abuse among their peers. Suggested activities include public service announcements, drinking and driving demonstrations, and a "dry" disco. The plans can be implemented in school or community settings.

375. National Institute on Alcohol Abuse and Alcoholism. ON THE SIDELINES: AN ADULT LEADER GUIDE FOR YOUTH ALCOHOL PROGRAMS. Prepared by Patricia Kassebaum, Bruce Hathaway, and Mary L. Mong. Washington, D.C.: U.S. Government Printing Office, 1981. 32 pp.

Suggests techniques and information resources for adult professionals or volunteers working with an alcohol prevention project for youth. Companion to no. 374 above (IS BEER A FOUR LETTER WORD?). Includes examples of short-term group projects, community outreach projects, and long-term peer programs.

376. National Institute on Alcohol Abuse and Alcoholism. PREVENTING ALCOHOL PROBLEMS THROUGH A STUDENT ASSISTANCE PROGRAM: A MANUAL FOR IMPLEMENTATION BASED ON THE WESTCHESTER COUNTY, NEW YORK, MODEL. Washington, D.C.: U.S. Government Printing Office, 1984. 35 pp. plus appendixes.

Describes the Westchester County, New York, student assistance program to provide intervention and prevention services for high school students with possible drug or alcohol problems (or whose parents may be drug or alcohol abusers). Discusses the goals, functions, and structure of the program and presents guidelines for planning and implementation (including funding and community support). There are also sections dealing with the qualifications and duties of student assistance counselors as well as the methods of referral to the program. Appendixes contain a sample program policy, federal regulations regarding confidentiality of client records, resource lists of state alcohol authoritites and prevention network members, and program evaluation forms. A bibliography of suggested reading is included.

377. National Institute on Alcohol Abuse and Alcoholism. PREVENTION PLUS: INVOLVING SCHOOLS, PARENTS, AND THE COMMUNITY IN ALCOHOL AND DRUG EDUCATION. Washington, D.C.: U.S. Government Printing Office, 1983. 324 pp.

Examines programs which have proved effective in preventing or dealing with alcohol and drug problems among youth. The programs described include classroom education and teacher training, parent education, and community prevention approaches, as well as school-based intervention approaches designed to help identify and deal with alcohol and drug problems. Also included are guidelines for developing school alcohol and drug policies. Objectives, sample activities, and lists of resource materials are included for each program. Further prevention ideas and programs are briefly described in the appendixes.

378. National Institute on Alcohol Abuse and Alcoholism. TEACHING ABOUT DRINKING. Washington, D.C.: U.S. Government Printing Office, 1978. 10 pp.

Booklet offers suggestions to help teachers provide information and handle classroom situations regarding alcohol use. Emphasizes the influence of teacher attitudes and adult role modeling on adolescent alcohol use.

379. National Institute on Alcohol Abuse and Alcoholism. THE WHOLE COLLEGE CATALOG ABOUT DRINKING. Washington, D.C.: U.S. Government Printing Office, 1976. 129 pp.

Provides information and examples to help plan and implement a college alcohol abuse program. Included are basic facts about alcohol use and abuse, guidelines for needs assessment and evaluation, a variety of suggested program approaches, and descriptions of eighteen operating campus programs.

380. O'Gorman, Patricia. THE PUBLIC HEALTH MODEL OF PREVENTION. Minneapolis: Johnson Institute, 1983. 24 pp.

Discusses various approaches that have been used to prevent alcohol and drug abuse and outlines a public health prevention model based on a combination of strategies. Contains guidelines for determining high-risk groups and for formulating a successful prevention approach based on supply strategies (regulating access to alcohol and making the physical environment safer for drinkers) and demand stategies (alcohol education programs in the schools and public education campaigns to provide information about alcohol use).

381. Operation Cork. WINTHROP AND MUNCHIE TALK ABOUT ALCOHOL. Santa Ynez, Calif.: Operation Cork, 1983. 16 pp.

Uses coloring-book format to present information about alcohol as a drug that affects the functioning of the brain and body. Avoids judgmental overtones about personal decisions on alcohol use. Suitable for elementary school children.

382. Parham, Philip A., with Patricia Merrill. THE CHURCH AND ALCOHOL: A RESOURCE MANUAL. San Antonio, Tex.: San Antonio Council on Alcoholism, 1983. 118 pp.

Designed to help clergy and adult church members provide alcohol education, alcoholism prevention, and help for alcoholics and their families. Focuses on the need to present accurate, unbiased information about alcohol use (moderate and heavy) and related problems. Includes materials to be used in counseling alcoholic families as well as discussions of the spiritual basis of Alcoholics Anonymous and its usefulness to the church. Also provides training materials for adults who will be teaching adolescent alcohol education classes in the church. Includes a variety of sample materials (handouts, questionnaires, etc.) and resource lists. Originally developed as an interdenominational project by the San Antonio Council on Alcoholism and local area churches.

383. Ray, Oakley. DRUGS, SOCIETY, AND HUMAN BEHAVIOR. 3d ed. St. Louis: C.V. Mosby Co., 1983. 512 pp.

Presents information on the physiological and social consequences of mood-altering drugs. The chapter on alcohol is included in the section on non-drugs (nicotine, caffeine, over-the-counter drugs, contraceptives). Production, consumption, and regulation of beverage alcohol are placed in a historical context leading up to a discussion of current trends. Effects of alcohol on the body (particularly the central nervous system) and several different alcoholism treatment approaches are also discussed. Other sections of the book cover psychotherapeutic drugs, narcotic drugs, and "phantasticants" (hallucinogens, marijuana, hashish). Originally designed as a college text but also helpful for the general reader.

384. Roberts, Clay, and Carol Mooney. HERE'S LOOKING AT YOU. Seattle: Comprehensive Health Education Foundation, 1975. 411 pp.

Provides a comprehensive alcohol education curriculum in multimedia format for grades k-12. Includes teacher's guide with seven kits of accompanying materials (books, games, charts, posters, puppets, and other items) for use at different grade levels. Teacher's guide outlines objectives for each grade level and presents learning activities with guidelines for the instructor. Content focuses on facts about alcohol and alcohol abuse, responsible decision making regarding alcohol use, coping skills, and self-concept. Materials for training teachers to successfully implement this program are also available.

385. Russell, Robert D. WHAT SHALL WE TEACH THE YOUNG ABOUT DRINKING? Popular Pamphlets on Alcohol Problems, No. 5. New Brunswick, N.J.: Rutgers Center of Alcohol Studies, 1970. 14 pp.

Presents a quick overview for educators on the main facets of alcohol education. Offers suggestions on course content (primarily focused on metabolism of alcohol, effects of alcohol on the body, drinking behavior, and development of alcoholism) and an analysis of the relationship between content and social context. Includes a brief reading list.

386. Sheppard, Margaret A., Michael S. Goodstadt, Gloria Torrance, and Marlo Fieldstone. ALCOHOL EDUCATION: TEN LESSON PLANS FOR GRADES 9 AND 10. Toronto: Addiction Research Foundation, 1978. 83 pp.

Contains lesson plans for use with ninth and tenth grade students on alcohol use and its effects. Topics include alcohol and myths, alcohol and needs (physical, emotional, intellectual), alcohol and the law, alcohol and driving, alcohol and the family, alcohol and fitness, and alcohol and sexuality. There are values clarification exercises, sample group and individual projects, and suggestions for additional print and audiovisual materials.

(Similar to item no. 387 below; both guides may be used alone or with supplementary materials.)

387. Sheppard, Margaret A., Michael S.Goodstadt, Gloria Torrance, and Marlo Fieldstone. ALCOHOL EDUCATION: TEN LESSON PLANS FOR GRADES 7 AND 8. Toronto: Addiction Research Foundation, 1978. 58 pp.

Provides lesson plans with discussion questions and research topics for use with seventh and eighth grade students. Covers a variety of aspects of alcohol use including alcohol and advertising, effects of drinking, driving and drinking, positive uses of alcohol, teenage use of alcohol, alcohol and the family, and alcohol and athletics. Presents factual information about alcohol as well as values clarification exercises to promote responsible decision making about alcohol use.

388. Smith, Roy H. A CURRICULUM FOR ALCOHOL EDUCATION. Washington, D.C.: University Press of America, 1981. 203 pp.

Designed for use in education courses for drunk drivers or problem drinkers. There are two curricula, each divided into eight sessions that may be used individually or in any combination. The first curriculum deals primarily with alcohol use and highway safety and includes information on the effects of alcohol on driving skills, drinking customs and societal attitudes, and the long-term consequences of heavy alcohol use. The second curriculum is intended for people who are experiencing any problems as a result of their drinking. The sessions focus on self-examination of alcohol use and behavioral change toward abstinence or controlled drinking. Each session provides content information for the group leader as well as an outline for presenting the material, suggested activities, and a brief list of content reources (print and audiovisual materials).

389. Smithers, Christopher D., Foundation. IT'S ALL RIGHT TO SAY "THANKS, I DON'T DRINK." Mill Neck, N.Y.: Christopher D. Smithers Foundation, n.d. 2 pp.

Provides information about why individuals may not wish to drink alcoholic beverages and offers suggestions for those who want to refuse drinks. Also discusses the role of the church and the minister in preventing or identifying alcohol problems among the congregation.

390. Tans, Mary D., ed. GETTING THE WORD OUT. Madison: Wisconsin Clearinghouse, 1979. 74 pp.

Presentation of practical guidelines for planning and implementing a public awareness campaign for an agency or program. Includes suggestions for evaluating resources, reaching "hard to reach" audiences, and changing attitudes. Also discusses how various media resources (newspapers, radio and television, brochures, etc.) may be used most effectively. This approach could be helpful for school and community alcohol prevention programs. There is a short bibliography of alcohol and drug materials as well as a list of organizations for further information.

391. United States Brewers Association. CHEERS! SIX KEYS TO OPERATING RESPONSIBLE PUBS. Washington, D.C.: United States Brewers Association, n.d. 2 pp.

Offers suggestions to help college pub personnel promote responsible drinking practices. Focuses on the pub as a center for social interaction rather than simply a place to drink.

392. United States Jaycees, Operation Threshold. ALL IN THE FAMILY. Tulsa, Okla.: United States Jaycees, 1975. 46 pp. (plus 20 pp. chairman's guide).

Provides a framework for discussion among parents, families, or larger groups on teaching children about responsible alcohol use (including abstention). Focuses on parental role modeling and communication of values and attitudes toward alcohol use. Includes self-tests for adults, parents, and teenagers about alcohol use. A chairman's guide to facilitate large group discussions is available.

See also: 3, 4, 5, 7, 19, 20, 52, 243, 255, 256, 354.

16. LEGAL AND SOCIAL ISSUES

Materials dealing with public policy or legislation regarding alcohol use are covered in this chapter. In addition, there are several overviews of the effects of alcohol use on society and the responsibilities of citizens and government to deal with alcohol-related problems. There are also items concerning the legal rights of the alcoholic as well as the responsibilities of the attorney with an alcoholic client. For materials related to alcohol use and traffic safety, see chapter fourteen.

393. Beauchamp, Dan E. BEYOND ALCOHOLISM: ALCOHOL AND PUBLIC HEALTH POLICY. Philadelphia: Temple University Press, 1980. 222 pp.

Describes the evolution of public policy toward alcohol use since the end of Prohibition. Recommends a public health approach that includes reasonable restrictions on availability and consumption of alcohol, education about alcohol use and effects, and treatment for alcohol problems.

394. Carnahan, William A. LEGAL ISSUES AFFECTING EMPLOYEE ASSISTANCE PROGRAMS. Arlington, Va.: Association of Labor-Management Administrators and Consultants on Alcoholism, 1984. 27 pp.

Identifies and describes (using actual case examples) those legal issues which may be of concern to companies providing employee assistance programs (EAPs) to deal with alcohol or other personal problems affecting employees' work performance. Explains federal and state-level regulations that deal with licensing of treatment personnel and facilities as well as confidentiality of client records. Also discusses other areas--treatment diagnosis, employee discipline, drug and alcohol screening--where unions or company management may have legal rights or responsiblities.

395. Carrithers, Richard C. THE ALCOHOLIC CLIENT. Newport Beach, Calif.: CompCare Publications, n.d. 15 pp.

Practical guidelines to help attorneys identify clients with alcohol problems and refer them for help. Discusses some of the legal problems that motivate alcoholics to seek counsel and also describes some of the behavioral signs of alcoholism. Includes a sample letter for establishing a referral system between attorneys and local treatment resources.

396. Evans, David G. A PRACTITIONER'S GUIDE TO ALCOHOLISM AND THE LAW. Center City, Minn.: Hazelden, 1983. 91 pp.

Presentation of basic information to help alcoholism practitioners (counselors, treatment program administrators), attorneys, and law enforcement personnel deal with legal issues regarding alcoholics and their families. Topics discussed include malpractice in the handling and treatment of alcoholics, the application of confidentiality laws and regulations to alcoholism, intoxication or alcoholism as a defense in criminal cases, family law as applied to divorce and domestic violence in alcoholic situations, and employment issues (discrimination, employee assistance programs). There is also a section to help attorneys identify and deal with cases involving alcohol problems. Information is concise and easy to understand and could be used by alcoholics or laypersons who have legal questions about alcohol issues.

397. Hazelden Foundation. IF YOU DRINK, WHAT YOU SHOULD KNOW AND DO. Center City, Minn.: Hazelden, n.d. 8 pp.

Summarizes the main areas of individual and social responsibility of alcohol users. Offers guidelines for self-evaluation of drinking behavior, helping children make responsible decisions about alcohol use, and responsibility of hosts who serve alcoholic beverages. Includes a blood alcohol chart for determining level of impairment after alcohol use.

398. Jacobson, Michael, Robert Atkins, and George Hacker. THE BOOZE MERCHANTS: THE INEBRIATING OF AMERICA.

Washington, D.C.: Center for Science in the Public Interest, 1983. 159 pp.

Exploration of the ways in which alcoholic beverage manufacturers target their advertising toward specific groups, including new or light drinkers (youth, women). Discusses the various themes--success, adventure, sexuality--that are projected in media ads and suggests ways in which greater control can be exercised over the content and amount of alcohol advertising.

399. Kirsch, Nathan S. IN TROUBLE WITH ALCOHOL AND THE LAW: A MANUAL FOR JUDGES AND ATTORNEYS. Trenton: New Jersey State Division of Alcoholism, 1980. 40 pp.

Provides information to help judges and attorneys identify and deal effectively with clients who have drinking problems. Symptoms of an alcohol problem, such as denial and compulsion to drink, are described as well as some consequences which may lead the alcohol-troubled person into difficulty with the law--drunk driving, violent behavior, disorderly conduct. Various legal options available in New Jersey to coerce the client into an alcohol treatment program are reviewed. There is also a brief section describing the rights of the alcoholic offender, including confidentiality and non-discrimination in employment.

400. Luks, Allan. WILL AMERICA SOBER UP? Boston: Beacon Press, 1983. 212 pp.

Presents information and suggestions designed to reduce alcohol abuse and to help Americans moderate their drinking practices. Advocates such public strategies as a national alcohol education campaign, increased federal interference (such as higher alcohol taxes), and legislation to identify and coerce alcoholics into treatment. Includes data from a 1982 Gallup Poll on drinking patterns and problems.

401. National Institute on Alcohol Abuse and Alcoholism. FIFTH SPECIAL REPORT TO THE U.S. CONGRESS ON ALCOHOL AND HEALTH FROM THE SECRETARY OF HEALTH AND HUMAN SERVICES. Washington, D.C.: U.S. Government Printing Office, 1983. 146 pp.

Examines the contemporary state of the nation's health regarding alcohol use, including psychological, physiological, and social consequences of alcohol abuse. Covers alcohol consumption patterns and prevalence of alcohol problems among various population groups, genetic and environmental factors in alcoholism, cognitive and neurological effects of alcohol use, medical consequences of alcohol use on various body systems, and the effects of alcohol on the developing fetus (including fetal alcohol syndrome). The section on social consequences looks at the relationships between alcohol and crime (including violent crime such as rape), alcohol and suicide, alcohol and accidents, and alcohol and family disruption. Treatment issues, such as early diagnosis, treatment settings, and various therapeutic approaches, are also discussed along with a review of prevention approaches--both educational and legislative. References and index are included. This is the latest in this series of reports issued irregularly since 1971.

402. New York City Affiliate of the National Council on Alcoholism and the Legal Action Center of the City of New York. THE RIGHTS OF ALCOHOLICS AND THEIR FAMILIES. New York: New York Affiliate of the National Council on Alcoholism and the Legal Action Center of the City of New York, 1982. 40 pp.

Explains the legal rights of active and recovered alcoholics. Covers such topics as confidentiality of treatment records, alcoholism and criminal responsibility, domestic relations, driving while intoxicated, employment, licensing, credit, insurance coverage, public assistance, enforced treatment, and veterans benefits. Includes explanations of federal and New York State laws. Helpful for social workers, treatment personnel, attorneys, government agencies, and any persons involved with alcoholics or their families.

403. Royce, James E. ALCOHOL AND RESPONSIBILITY. Center City, Minn.: Hazelden, 1979. 21 pp.

Discusses the issue of moral responsibility in alcoholism. Examines historical attitudes toward drinking and alcoholism as well as the modern understanding of alcoholism as an illness. Distinguishes the choice involved in nonalcoholic drinking and drunkenness from the lack of control inherent in alcoholism.

404. Wechsler, Henry, ed. MINIMUM-DRINKING-AGE LAWS: AN EVALUATION. Lexington, Mass.: Lexington Books, 1980. 187 pp.

Examines the use and effectiveness of drinking-age laws in controlling alcohol use by young people. Explores the relationship of drinking age to traffic accidents, youthful drinking practices, and admissions to treatment for alcohol problems. There is a helpful summary of research findings and suggestions for future areas of investigation.

405. Weinberg, Jon R. HELPING THE CLIENT WITH ALCOHOL-RELATED PROBLEMS. Minneapolis: CompCare Publications, n.d. 15 pp.

Advises attorneys on how to recognize alcohol-related problems in their clients. Contains guidelines for obtaining information through client interviews about drinking patterns and consequences and offers suggestions for motivating the client toward alcoholism treatment. Discusses divorce and criminal cases.

See also: 26, 350.

APPENDIX A

Alcohol-Related Periodicals

*(Denotes emphasis on research material)

A.A. Grapevine
468 Park Ave. South
New York, N.Y. 10016
1944-- monthly

The Addiction Letter
Manisses Communications Group
P.O. Box 3357
Wayland Square
Providence, R.I. 02906-0357
1985-- monthly

Alcohol Awareness Service
National Clearinghouse for Alcohol Information
Dept. AAS
P.O. Box 2345
Rockville, Md. 20852
1981-- bimonthly

***Alcohol Clinical Update**
Project Cork
Dartmouth Medical School
Hanover, N.H. 03756
1982-- bimonthly

***Alcohol Health and Research World**
Superintendent of Documents
U.S. Government Printing Office
Washington, D.C. 20402
1973-- quarterly

Alcoholism Report
Manisses Communications Group
P.O. Box 3357
Wayland Square
Providence, R.I. 02906-0357
1972-- semimonthly

Alcoholism/The National Magazine
Alcom, Inc.
P.O. Box 19519
Seattle, Wash. 98109
1980-- bimonthly

***Alcoholism Treatment Quarterly**
Haworth Press
28 East 22nd St.
New York, N.Y. 10010
1984-- quarterly

COA Review
Thomas Perrin, Inc.
P.O. Box 423
Rutherford, N.J. 07070
1983-- bimonthly

***Drinking and Drug Practices Surveyor**
Alcohol Research Group
1816 Scenic Ave.
Berkeley, Calif. 94709
1970-- irregular

EAP Digest
Performance Resource Press, Inc.
2145 Crooks Rd.
Suite 103
Troy, Mich. 48084
1980-- bimonthly

Focus on Family and Chemical Dependency
U.S. Journal of Drug and Alcohol Dependence
1721 Blount Rd.
Suite #1
Pompano Beach, Fla. 33069
1978-- bimonthly
(formerly titled **Focus on Alcohol and Drug Issues**)

Forum
Al-Anon Family Group Headquarters, Inc.
1 Park Ave.
New York, N.Y. 10016
1951-- monthly

The Journal
Addiction Research Foundation
33 Russell St.
Toronto, Ontario M5S 2S1
Canada
1972-- monthly

Journal of Alcohol and Drug Education
Alcohol and Drug Problems Association of North America
1120 East Oakland
P.O. Box 10212
Lansing, Mich. 48901
1955-- three times per year

***Journal of Studies on Alcohol**
Rutgers Center of Alcohol Studies
P.O. Box 969
Piscataway, N.J. 08854
1940-- bimonthly

U.S. Journal of Drug and Alcohol Dependence
1721 Blount Rd.
Suite #1
Pompano Beach, Fla. 33069
1977-- monthly

APPENDIX B

Resource Organizations

I. Information (including research, education and training, and general information) on alcohol and related problems:

Addiction Research Foundation
33 Russell St.
Toronto, Ontario M5S 2S1
Canada
(416) 595-6144

Alcohol Research Group
1816 Scenic Ave.
Berkeley, Calif. 94709
(415) 642-5208

Alcoholism and Drug Abuse Institute
3937 15th Ave., N.E.
Seattle, Wash. 98105
(206) 543-0937

National Clearinghouse for Alcohol Information
P.O. Box 2345
Rockville, Md. 20852
(301) 468-2600

National Council on Alcoholism
12 West 21st St.
7th Floor
New York, N.Y. 10010
(212) 206-6770

National Institute on Alcohol Abuse and Alcoholism
U.S. Dept. of Health and Human Services
5600 Fishers Lane
Rockville, Md. 20857
(301) 443-3885

National Safety Council
444 North Michigan Ave.
Chicago, Ill. 60611
(312) 527-4800

Prevention Resource Center
2532 Durant Ave.
Berkeley, Calif. 94704
(415) 486-1111

Project Cork Resource Center
Dept. of Psychiatry
Dartmouth Medical School
Hanover, N.H. 03755
(603) 646-7540

Rutgers Center of Alcohol Studies
P.O. Box 969
Piscataway, N.J. 08854
(201) 932-2190

II. For alcoholics and their families:

Al-Anon Family Group Headquarters, Inc.
P.O. Box 182
Madison Square Station
New York, N.Y. 10159-0182
(212) 481-6565

Alcoholics Anonymous (A.A.)
General Service Office
P.O. Box 459
Grand Central Station
New York, N.Y. 10163
(212) 686-1100

Children of Alcoholics Foundation
540 Madison Ave.
23rd Floor
New York, N.Y. 10022
(212) 980-5394

National Association for Children of Alcoholics
P.O. Box 421691
San Francisco, Calif. 94142
(415) 431-1366

Operation Cork
8939 Villa La Jolla Dr.
Suite 203
San Diego, Calif. 92037
(714) 452-5716

Women for Sobriety, Inc.
Box 618
Quakerstown, Pa. 18951
(215) 536-8026

III. Professional and trade associations:

Association of Labor-Management Administrators and Consultants on Alcoholism, Inc.
1800 North Kent St.
Arlington, Va. 22209
(703) 522-6272

Distilled Spirits Council of the United States, Inc.
1250 I St., N.W.
Suite 900
Washington, D.C. 20005
(202) 628-3544

Licensed Beverage Information Council
425 13th St., N.W.
Suite 1300
Washington, D.C. 20004
(202) 628-3544

National Association of Lesbian and Gay Alcoholism Professionals
1208 East State Blvd.
Fort Wayne, Ind. 46805
(219) 483-8280

Substance Abuse Librarians and Information Specialists
c/o Andrea Mitchell
Alcohol Research Group
1816 Scenic Ave.
Berkeley, Calif. 94702
(415) 642-5208

United States Brewers Association, Inc.
1750 K St., N.W.
Washington, D.C. 20006
(202) 466-2400

Wine Institute
165 Post St.
San Francisco, Calif. 94108
(415) 986-0878

IV. Special focus groups:

BACCUS (Boost Alcohol Consciousness Concerning the Health of University Students) of the U. S., Inc.
c/o Campus Alcohol Information Center
124 Tigert Hall
University of Florida
Gainesville, Fla. 32611
(904) 392-1261

Mothers Against Drunk Drivers (MADD)
5530 Primrose
Suite 146
Fair Oaks, Calif. 95628
(916) 966-MADD

National Black Alcoholism Council
417 South Dearborn St.
Suite 1000
Chicago, Ill. 60605
(312) 663-5780

National Clergy Council on Alcoholism
3112 7th St., N.E.
Washington, D.C. 20017
(202) 832-3211

North Conway Institute
14 Beacon St.
Boston, Mass. 02108
(617) 742-0424

Remove Intoxicated Drivers (RID)
P.O. Box 520
Schenectady, N.Y. 12301
(518) 372-0034

Students Against Driving Drunk (SADD)
Box 800
Marlboro, Mass. 01752
(617) 481-3568

Author Index

Title Index